COUNTRY LIVING

750

Great Ideas *for* Decorating *on a* Budget

Transform Your Home Inside & Out

from the Editors of
Country Living Magazine
Text by Ray Furse

Hearst Books
A Division of Sterling Publishing Co., Inc.
New York

Library of Congress Cataloging-in-Publication Data is available.

First Paperback Edition 2005.
Published by Hearst Books
A Division of Sterling Publishing Co., Inc.
387 Park Avenue South, New York, NY 10016

Country Living and Hearst Books are trademarks of Hearst Communications, Inc.

Distributed in Canada by Sterling Publishing
c/o Canadian Manda Group, 165 Dufferin Street
Toronto, Ontario, Canada M6K 3H6

Distributed in Australia by Capricorn Link (Australia) Pty. Ltd.
P.O. Box 704, Windsor, NSW 2756 Australia

Printed in China
All rights reserved

Sterling ISBN 13: 978-1-58816-304-2
ISBN 10: 1-58816-304-0

For Country Living
Editor-in-Chief: Nancy Mernit Soriano
Design Director: Susan M. Netzel
Executive Editor: Lawrence A. Bilotti

www.countryliving.com

Designed by Liz Trovato

10 9 8 7 6 5 4 3

For information about custom editions, special sales, premium and corporate purchases,
please contact Sterling Special Sales Department at 800-805-5489 or
specialsales@sterlingpub.com.

Contents

Introduction

Deciding to undertake some improvements in your home is the first step in an exciting but challenging process. Whether your goal is to make your space more functional or to create a look that suits your personal tastes, realizing your dreams can be frustrating when you're working within a limited budget. Sometimes it's also hard just knowing where—or how—to begin. This book is here to help.

Country Living: 750 Great Ideas for Decorating on a Budget offers solutions for transforming every room in your house without breaking the bank. The following pages provide valuable ideas for everything from seasonal makeovers to simple decorating projects for living rooms and bedrooms to affordable ways to renovate your kitchen or bathroom. You don't need to spend a fortune to achieve a stylish renovation—fabric, paint, and unexpected decorative details can work wonders in a space at a reasonable price. Flea markets and auctions are rich resources for vintage furniture and accessories, and yard sales can yield wonderful finds like antique pottery and quilts. Simplicity, warmth, and comfort have always been hallmarks of country style—this book shares a wealth of ideas for making that style accessible, no matter how limited your space or budget may be.

Country decor allows for mixing the old with the new and for expressing personal style. The ideas in this book will inspire you to do just that. As you begin this fun and creative undertaking, keep the following five basics in mind—and don't forget that when you approach a makeover with a little imagination, there are no limits to realizing your dreams!

Nancy Mernit Soriano

Editor-in-Chief, *Country Living* Magazine

❧ The Five Basics

1. Paint. Always the least expensive way to change the look of any space, and you can do it yourself. Go neutral or light in consideration of the colors to come.

2. Slipcovers. Custom or ready made (even cheaper) are a budget alternative to replacing worn furniture and making a tired room look new.

3. Fabrics. Don't hide those collections in a linen closet. Place them around for impact and consider making some contrasting or matching pillows.

4. Artwork. Again, most of us have more tucked away than we can display on our walls. Change is good.

5. Windows. There are literally thousands of budget window treatments available on-line or at retail stores. Changing the quality of light in a room will change its mood.

Kitchens

Our homes all probably have a space called a living room or family room, but we probably enjoy as many hours in the kitchen with our families as we do in that room. As the place where food is prepared and meals are shared, the country kitchen is an important gathering place for activities and chats throughout the day. Often, it's the most warm, cozy room in the house.

When redecorating a kitchen, ordering brand-new appliances and installing new countertops, fixtures, and floors is a tempting fantasy. However, most of us can't afford to outfit our dream kitchens from scratch. And even if we could, how would we balance the warmth and character of a country kitchen's wide-plank floors, beaded board walls, and comfortably worn, rustic cabinets with modern surfaces like stone and stainless steel? Whether you're planning to renovate or just redecorate, this chapter is full of ideas for mixing the old with the new, making the most of limited space, and creating your dream kitchen on a modest budget.

Improving on What You Have

6 Keep magazine articles that list low-cost sources for tile, cabinets, and countertops, and clip photos of appealing color schemes. Know where to get everything you need and how much it will cost. Make a spreadsheet and a schedule and abide by each to avoid disappointment.

7 Avoid a big bill by repainting old cabinets in good repair instead of replacing them. Here, the dark wooden cabinets were painted yellow-gold to brighten the room, while the glass-fronted doors were left for contrast.

8
If you need new cabinets, save money by ordering them unfinished and painting them yourself.

9
Paint and distress an already worn, well-used kitchen island to give it a country farmhouse look. Experiment on plywood to perfect your techniques.

10
Shop at flea markets for decorative iron pieces like this bracket mounted under the stove hood—they give traditional detail to the room affordably.

You don't necessarily have to replace old laminate cabinets—they can be painted. Ask at your most knowledgeable hardware store for a good primer that sticks well to such surfaces.

12

Even if the room is a hundred years old, if tackled with imagination, renovating a kitchen need not be a budget buster: cover imperfections on old wood floors with a sturdy, neutral rug.

13

Use beaded board, which retains a traditional look, to cover plaster walls that would be costly to repair.

14

Open shelving is often far more period-accurate than cabinets and it is far less expensive.

15

Cover a hopelessly degraded work surface with stain-and-water-resistant oilcloth in a colorful pattern.

16
Cover the front of your dishwasher with a cabinet panel to avoid an unsightly wall of appliances.

17
In a kitchen with a nice view, leave the window curtainless (and shutterless) to open up the room, let in more light, and make the space feel less cluttered.

18
A window-mounted glass shelf holding glassware allows a collection to be displayed without blocking precious light.

19
Oversized crown molding gives a kitchen a finished look and can also actually make it appear bigger.

20
A bamboo (or sea-grass) rug adds warmth to a kitchen and is an economical upgrade from a worn vinyl floor.

21 Bamboo, a grass that is harvested after four or five years' growth, is also used to make flooring as hard as maple at half its price.

22 With wood floors, especially in an old home, sometimes you have to accept what you've inherited. If a kitchen floor has taken so much wear and tear that even sanding and stripping won't help, paint it with a high-gloss enamel to give it a clean, bright look.

Giving a New Kitchen an Old Look

23 Making a brand-new kitchen addition match the style of an old house can be challenging. Search salvage yards for materials—they can be gold mines for everything from antique fixtures to ceiling beams.

24 Make inexpensive pine cabinets "antique" with a crackle-glaze finish that replicates an early nineteenth-century texture.

Soapstone counter-
tops are subdued in
color, easy to care
for, and they have
an unobtrusive
antique look.

26

Hide modern
appliances such as
a coffeemaker,
blender, and toaster
in an "appliance
garage" such as the
one in the corner.

27

Simple sheets of burlap diffuse early morning light and add to the period ambience.

28

Combined with other details, a collection of antique glassware can give your kitchen a charming, old-fashioned look.

Give low-cost **29** kitchen cabinets a traditional look by simply facing them with beaded-board paneling available from most home improvement centers.

Solutions for Storage and Workspace

30
Where space is at a premium, look for creative storage solutions. A faux partial wall next to the refrigerator here is in fact a slide-out storage rack.

Almost any old table can be repurposed for a kitchen island; look for the proper size, sturdiness, and deep drawers for storage. If you have some extra money in your budget and if necessary, the top can be supplemented with a layer of butcher block or slate cut to size.

32 If your budget allows, installing a kitchen island with an integrated cooktop (and down-drafted venting) frees up counter space near the sink and under cabinets.

33 To reduce visual clutter and give your kitchen a more spacious feel, leave one wall entirely free of cabinets.

34 If you install cabinets or shelves in a small kitchen, take them all the way to the top for extra storage—and then add a decorative stepstool so you can reach them.

35
A high, well-out-of-the-way wrap-around shelf is a good place to store large serving bowls or collections you don't want to hide behind cabinet doors.

36
Frosted-glass doors are a relatively inexpensive way to create visual space in a small kitchen while still concealing the contents of cabinets.

37
Building the microwave in under a cabinet minimizes clutter and leaves your countertops clear.

38 Opening up the kitchen to the dining area can create a larger, family-friendly space.

39 Open shelving displaying a collection of colorful yet practical bowls adds to the informality.

49

A neutral two-tone color scheme can make a small kitchen space seem larger, as can glass-fronted cabinets.

41 An under-sink storage unit mounted on the door holds everything you need when it's time to clean up.

42 A two-tiered cutlery divider doubles available drawer space while keeping contents accessible and neatly in place—the top tray slides easily over the bottom.

43 A sliding pantry-style cabinet provides extra storage without taking up a lot of room: this one is only nine inches wide but holds three deep shelves for storing bottles and canisters.

44 Mounting the microwave above the stove saves valuable working space.

45 Look for one of many clever new solutions for the perennial problem of cabinet clutter. Here, a wall-mounted stainless-steel spice rack helps minimize the problem.

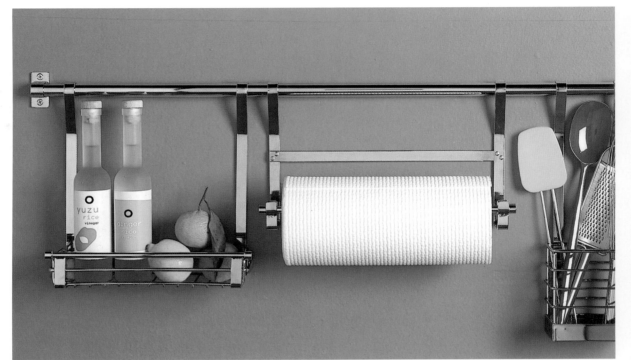

46 The kitchen—which most of the family visits frequently—is the ideal place for a message board. Mount a combination chalkboard/bulletin board and keep recipes, phone numbers, and to-do lists in one place—and off tables and countertops.

47 Tin picnic baskets with wooden handles found at flea markets not only provide colorful storage but are becoming valuable collectibles.

48 For a personal solution to family storage needs, assign each member a colorful basket to hold mail, messages, and odd and ends.

Making the Most of Great Finds

49 Suspend an antique garden gate from the kitchen ceiling to make an ornate pot-and-pan storage rack.

50 A forty-dollar flea-market farmhouse table makes a sturdy and spacious center island.

51 This farmhouse sink was assembled from a fifty-dollar sideboard, a salvage-yard marble slab, and a basic soap-stone potting-shed sink.

52

If you can't hide it, flaunt it: open shelving holds a Pop Art-inspired collection of household goods.

53

Repurposing can be thought of as using the imagination to save money. That antique napkin ring collection can make an elegant set of egg cups.

54

Vintage flea-market chairs painted in different pastel shades make for colorful and informal seating.

Paint an old bench and put it in a window to make an attractive indoor garden that will provide fresh herbs through the winter.

56
Repurposing is a powerful tool for the budget-minded decorator. Here, a repainted plant stand serves as a storage rack for vintage plates and bowls.

Collectibles and Decorative Details

57 Bright flowers fashioned from crepe paper and attached to a utilitarian pot-and-pan rack can brighten the whole kitchen.

58

Here a stenciled backsplash was created to imitate and accentuate the patterns of the china pieces displayed.

59

The space above a refrigerator is often overlooked; here, the homeowner's collection of cookbooks is displayed in a custom-built bookcase.

Open shelves not only display collections proudly, they can be installed much more inexpensively than closed cabinets.

61

Use an old wire bakery rack to show off your collections from all sides— even from below.

The easiest way to brighten a kitchen or another room is with a prominent display of your colorful collections. Vivid dishes and glassware are not only visually appealing, but also practical and affordable.

63

A display of silver platters hung on a wall near the dining table reflects light beautifully and creates a focal point above a sideboard.

64

Hang a collection of china plates in a cozy breakfast nook where they will be admired every morning.

Dining Rooms

Without a doubt, over the decades the formal dining room has lost ground to the family's preference for more lived-in spaces. We seem to eschew the dining room in favor of gathering around the table in an eat-in kitchen, relaxing in the comfortable chairs of a family room, or eating on the patio in fine weather. But when we plan special dinners for good friends or celebratory feasts that call for a touch of more formal communion, we still feel most at home in the dining room.

Of course, the holidays especially beckon us to the dining room. What would Thanksgiving be without our loved ones seated around the table (with the bird in plain view, of course) offering thanks? The early darkness of the winter holidays makes the cozy candlelit dining room the warmest place for our meals. And entertaining guests in style requires a dining room, perhaps only as an excuse to gather and appreciate ourselves not as individuals, but as a group of good friends.

Yet formality need not imply coldness, nor does tradition require forcing out fun. The best dining rooms are those in which we look forward to being seated, with a sense of accomodation, elegant or whimsical table settings, and the promise of being well fed. Creating this atmosphere—in which conversation flows and friendships deepen—will cost you nothing more than a little imagination.

Above and Beyond the Table

65

When authentic
pieces are too
pricey, reproduction
chests and chairs
can help restore a
classic room to its
traditional look
(this home dates
from 1675) within a
reasonable budget.

66
For a traditional look, use uncommon table coverings like coverlets and rugs. In the early nineteenth-century in America, people considered rugs too valuable to put on the floor. They often draped them on tabletops or beds instead.

67
Combining silk or dried flowers with fresh-cut bouquets and displays of fruit is a great way to reduce the cost of seasonal arrangements—mixing the two makes its almost impossible to tell replica from real.

68

Tablecloths are no longer a must. Keep your dining table light and natural with a table runner in soft, colorful fabric.

69

Brighten simple painted dining chairs with flirty, coordinating seat covers. Attach Velcro closures to make removal for laundering a snap.

This dining room armoire was created from an inexpensive, unassembled kit that was then custom-painted to enhance the room's color scheme.

71

Placed against a
plain wall, a rustic
screen door becomes
a surprising, witty, and
affordable piece of art.

72 Don't shy away from mismatched items—creative repurposing involves thinking outside the box. Different styles of chairs in a simple color palette can add interest and character to your dining space, and a lattice-backed potting table can double as a rustic buffet for serving.

73 Just visible behind the new table, an old shoe-factory rack is a lovely and functional choice for storing wines.

74 A vintage file cabinet makes a well-organized, handsome buffet table.

Use wall colors as the jumping-off point for accents in table linens and window treatments to bring a unified, coherent look to the room.

76

Small adjustments and subtle modifications such as new shades for lighting fixtures and a fresh flower arrangement can adapt the look of your dining room to the season.

Graceful Table Settings

77
Create a perfect floral display every time by choosing a single bloom as the focus of your arrangement: place it in the center. Clip the stems of the surrounding flowers a bit shorter than that of the center flower so the blooms create an arc or rainbow.

78
Use your personal floral arrangements as centerpieces for your table or to mark places, letting guests take them home as treasured souvenirs.

79 Imagination trumps the pocketbook when it comes to surprising and delightful table settings.

80 Here a diminutive pre-seeded flower pot is marked with the name of the guest. Let friendships bloom!

81

Cheery rickrack tied in back secures a rabbit place card to a cotton napkin.

A trio of tulips in a small bud vase marked with each guest's initial gives everyone a sense of personal recognition.

83 For an inexpensive but elegant floral place setting, slip a single perfect rose-bud under the bell of an inverted wine glass.

84 Personalize a place setting by writing the guest's name in elegant script with art-masking fluid on a one-by-six-inch strip of watercolor paper.

85 When dry, brush across the writing with colored drawing ink. To really impress, try matching the hue of the ink with that of the rose.

86
Candlesticks
can become
favors when
tied with a
lovely ribbon.

87
Find new uses for old treasures. Vintage glasses and napkins like these give a whimsical touch to holiday parties.

88
Head to your local flea market or thrift shop to find mixed flatware, assorted dessert plates, and quirky linens for the table.

89
Capitalize on your creative opportunities: use a flowerpot, for example, to serve flatware or rolled napkins.

Living Rooms

In many country homes, the living room is an inviting, central family space that combines elements of comfort and ease with valued collections, heirlooms, and elegant pieces. The living room is where we go to curl up in an armchair by the fire, but it's also the place we choose to entertain guests, hang treasured paintings, and display antiques.

How do you mix elegance with comfort in such a well-used, well-visited, multi-purpose room? Here are dozens of ideas for using color, mixing and matching fabric, and choosing furniture. These affordable yet priceless elements of country style—simplicity, unexpected details, subtle contrasts in texture, faded florals, natural fabrics, and soft, clean whites combined with pastel or earthy accents—will give your living room the perfect balance between form and function.

Big Changes on a Small Budget

If the floor is in poor condition, consider using a larger area rug and refurbishing only the portion of the floor the rug doesn't cover. You can find woodlike tile for less than three dollars per square foot.

Experts agree that the least expensive way to create a complete new look for a living room is through repainting.

Consider doing the painting yourself. If you don't have to shell out money to pay professionals, you'll probably spend under two hundred dollars, and using today's paints make this job fairly easy to master.

Choose a color you like and that you can live with. Yellows, creams, and light greens create a light and airy effect.

Avoid high-gloss paints, which tend to show off imper-fections in walls.

The grain and color of plain wooden floors can open up a room and add to its richness. Bare floor-boards can also make a room look more spacious.

Imagination is
the budget-minded
decorator's most
powerful tool.

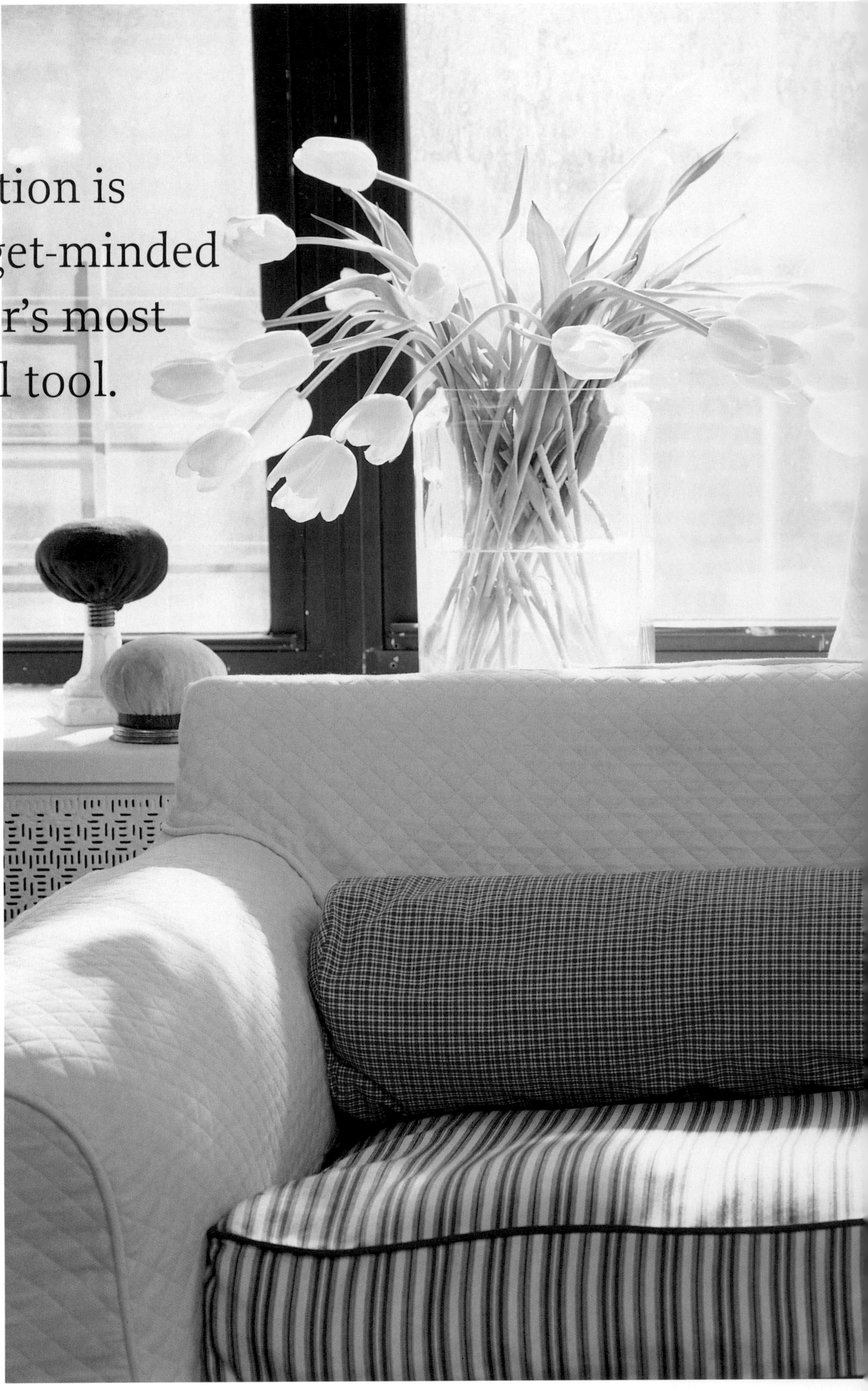

Replace or cover sectional cushions with a plump, down bench cushion for a cleaner, brighter look.

Increasing your decorating options by using double-sided, reversible curtains.

The life of a major purchase such as this cushiony chair can be dramatically increased by investing in a slipcover. Use it in the warmer months to brighten up the palette of your living room.

Ready made covers
are cheap enough so
that extra sets,
perhaps in a special
fabric or holiday
color, can be kept
on hand for when a
fresh or festive look
is called for.

101

If the renovation budget seems inadequate, don't despair. This homeowner saved money by searching salvage yards for period doors and windows rather than using custom-crafted replicas.

102

Sturdy but outdated armchairs and sofas were updated by reupholstering them with fabrics from an outlet store.

A dramatic and inexpensive redecoration of your living room can be achieved by slip-covering worn sofas and chairs rather than reupholstering or buying new pieces.

Installing built-in bookshelves with molding is an easy and inexpensive way of adding architectural distinction to any room.

105
Imperfect pieces help personalize a home. Chairs and a coffee table purchased at an antique fair give a lived-in look to the living room in this new modular home.

106
A new house can also benefit from traditional details. Crown moldings, dark-stained pine-plank floors, and an antique pressed-tin panel added to the fireplace mantel can make a just-built house look like it has stood for a century or more.

HARLEM LOST AND FOUND ADAMS / ROO

If gatherings typically happen in the kitchen and the living room is neglected, add a table for games in a corner to make it a more desirable space for shared activities.

108 Sometimes it's best to leave certain details alone. This heavily worn but still functional stair rail is part of the home's long history.

109 When living space is tight, minimizing just-for-show items can be a good policy. Keep out what you use most regularly.

Modestly priced cabinets for hiding the clutter of your audio and video equipment now come in every imaginable size and style.

Renovating with Color

Pastels are welcoming in any room. Pinks, lavenders, blues, and greens all readily lend themselves to restful and romantic themes.

Palette

112

Changing the colors in your living room is the most cost-effective way to give it a dramatic makeover. Whether you're painting walls or buying slipcovers, get swatches and test your palette before you introduce major changes.

113

Most colors have warm and cool traits. Warmer colors like pumpkin and berry will make your living room feel intimate and secure, while cooler shades like periwinkle blue contribute to a calming, restful atmosphere.

114

Consider the effects of color from room to room. Complementary colors, like various shades of yellow, will unify a decor, while contrasting colors, like yellow and red, will add depth and drama. A single trim color used throughout can help unite adjoining rooms.

Using white is, of course, a tried and true trick for making a small space appear larger.

Layer shades of
the same color.
Variations in hue
and intensity help
to separate them
naturally.

If layering seems
too daring, try
introducing a
contrasting color
for balance.

Stencils are an easy, affordable way to add elegant details to walls or to recreate the designs of expensive, ornate wall coverings.

Leave multiple layers of distressed paint in selected places to provide visual interest and to reveal a bit of your home's history.

Collections and accessories also contribute to a room's overall appeal. A cherished piece of artwork or an heirloom rug can be a great starting point when choosing a palette.

Painting a floor with a solid color or a pattern can create a dramatic focal point for a room.

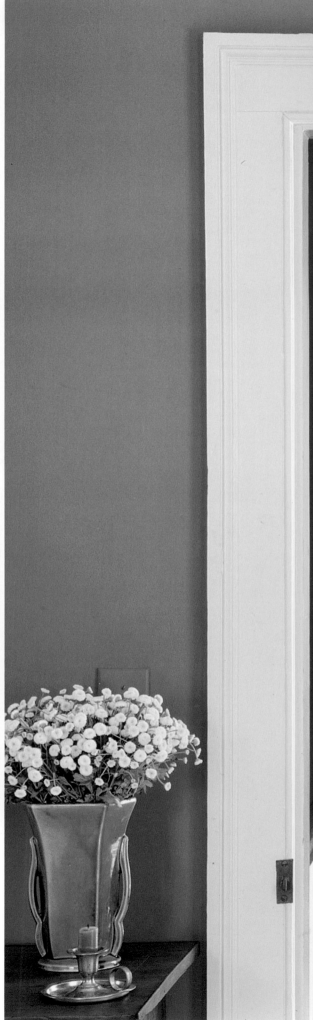

To draw the eye from room to room, repeat a trim color as the main color in a nearby room, or successively change the tint of paints in adjacent spaces.

Don't shy away from bold colors in small spaces. If a color seems too strong, you can always take it down a notch by using a lighter shade or by applying white trim.

This room maintains a subtle balance of color and pattern. Buttery walls maintain a familiar warmth, small pieces provide black accents, while the rugs and antique textiles introduce contrasting textures.

Framed silhouettes of family members make wonderful details in a room defined by black.

Although black is often associated with high-fashion chic, at heart it is basic and utilitarian. Against white it can help ground, define, and unify, and it can also bring out the best in other colors.

Decorating with the Seasons

Layers of warming fabric can make the indoors cozier come winter. Replace a breezy summer tablecloth or slip-cover with a heavier flannel throw.

You can probably do a complete seasonal redecoration with the fabrics you already own. Ward off the impending winter chill by bringing out woolens of all sorts.

Nubby wool throws and pillows in natural hues suggest both tranquillity and the season's changing moods.

Changing a living room's dark winter palette to a lighter one that welcomes spring doesn't require an expensive renovation. These two rooms have the same basic furniture items: frames and a table, chair, and lamp. But modestly priced items like new wallpaper, a slipcover, a tablecloth, and a pale lampshade transformed the first room (this page) to give it the fresh spring look you see in the second room (opposite page).

If repainting or repapering an entire room is not in your budget, try just doing one wall—stripes impart a cheerful, cottage-inspired style.

Hanging empty frames can create an "open window" effect that looks wonderful and graphic against playful stripes.

Covering a table and chairs with light fabrics brightens the whole room. Put flowers in a shiny bucket to accentuate the colorful details of the fabric.

Seasonal changes can be reflected in the look of your home without spending a lot of money. Small adjustments and subtle modifications—new lampshades, tabletop treatments, and fresh flower arrangements—will often do the trick.

Don't be afraid to layer. A sisal rug that protects a wooden floor through the year can be topped with a richly patterned, Persian wool carpet to provide added coziness in winter.

Antique throws and quilts used throughout a room add color and warmth.

Artwork can transform bleak winter views, and a mirror over the mantel can warm and open up the room.

128

Slide off winter's ring-top floral curtains and replace them with lighter colors or tie-top panels.

129

Simple black frames can help unify different styles of fine art and photos.

Boxy, down-filled floor cushions make for casual seating in the warmer seasons.

Use the abundant fruits and fresh flowers of summer to add color to the living room, either by using print slipcovers or by including arrangements on tables and mantels.

Unexpected Details

A windowless wall made this room dark until the owners found an antique pediment and porch columns and installed them to frame a nearly full-wall mirror.

Don't be afraid to mix and match whimsical elements. The important thing, as in composing a still life painting, is to balance color and scale.

Old game boards, which can be obtained at flea markets, are as visually arresting as any expensive framed work of art.

A decorative row of antique portraits can engage our interest and take us on a quick journey back in time.

146

Stencils can stand in (unexpectedly) for something expected.

A vintage stepladder
can be repurposed
to make an informal
plant stand.

148

For a surprising and colorful table surface, cover an unframed painting with a pane of glass.

A three-layer stack of striped suitcases from the 1930s and 1940s creates an attractive end table.

Vintage luggage, a fairly common flea market offering, can be used in interesting ways.

Period paper labels like those on this 1920s wooden hat box make an interesting focal point.

Vintage luggage like this steamer trunk can recall both bygone days and far-away places, and it makes a handsome, although informal, endtable when closed.

Reproduction game boards and vintage game pieces make great table accents.

Inexpensive Accents

154

A thrifty way to add color and interest to plain spaces is to hang or display the colorful china collection you probably have stacked in a cabinet somewhere.

155

Wall hangers for all sizes and shapes of china can be readily found in your local hardware store.

156

Use one key design element—in this case, flowers—to bring a collection together and project a common theme.

Suspend a pair of plates in contrasting colors by threading two lengths of wide, sturdy ribbon through a curtain ring, forming a loop. Tie the ends in a bow and hang from a hook.

158 Try clustering antique and new, and traditional and contemporary pieces around a central platter.

159 Join two lengths of wood to make a bookend (or find one made in a flea market). Then chisel a groove down the center of each bookend in which to nestle a colorful plate.

Make a small space feel larger, brighten a dim corner, or simply indulge your vanity by covering an entire wall with framed mirrors.

Search flea markets for inexpensive mirrors of varying size and shape. Don't worry about finding perfect glass—wavy reflections can prove much more interesting.

Paint the frames the same color to unify the presentation and call attention to their different designs.

Hang the mirrors at different levels, from waist high all the way to the ceiling.

Candles can be both soothing and invigorating, offering a boost to the spirit as well as a relaxing ambience.

Candles also have the power to enhance your seasonal decor, adding to the festivity of the holidays. Use them on a mantelpiece, table, or virtually any (safe) place you want to create some soft, welcoming holiday atmosphere.

A scented candle not only gives light, but also offers a delicate touch of fragrance to the living room.

For perfect burning, trim the candle's wick to just the right length, about one-quarter inch, before lighting. Don't lift or move a burning candle; snuff it out and wait until the wax has cooled.

Bedrooms

 Your bedroom is your private retreat, an inspirational haven that provides comfort and solace from the hectic everyday world and speaks of the personality that inhabits it. But with so many enticing choices in the world of bedding, paint, and accessories, how do you begin to fashion the bedroom dreams are made of?

To help you get started, we present a number of imaginative rooms with tips on how to get those looks on a modest budget. Use these as starting points and let them inspire you to infuse your own retreat with personal style. Sweet dreams!

Must-Haves for Easy Bedroom Makeovers

168
A budget bedroom makeover can be accomplished by simply fine-tuning color and accessories.

169
For bed linens, try an upbeat palette of pale pink and lavender, soothing green, or buttery yellow.

170
A neutral background sets off and emphasizes cosmetic changes.

Vintage linens,
another flea market
item, often seem
richer and cozier
than their modern
counterparts,
although fitted
sheets are still the
most convenient
base.

172
Blanket chests, trunks, or hope chests add a traditional country look to bedrooms and are also great places to store quilts and blankets at the foot of the bed.

173
Use restful colors. The white walls and pale gray woodwork here accentuate the warm tones of the wooden furniture, creating a cozy and quiet space.

174

A bedroom needs ample storage. If closet space is not sufficient, look for tall dressers or bureaus with deep drawers at flea markets—you don't have to spend a lot, especially if you are skilled at refinishing or painting furniture.

175

For an alternate quick and inexpensive bedroom makeover, have a selection of colorful bed linens to choose from. Mix white sheets and pillowcases with bright floral sheets and pillowcases. Choose a quilt made from vintage fabric in complementary colors to layer at the foot of the bed and voila!

176

Let a treasured quilt or bedspread be the focus of the bedroom: use accents that complement and showcase its design and color.

177

Paint a simple pine bench and place it at the foot of your bed for keeping warm blankets handy.

178

Drape sheer curtain panels over a wall-mounted bracket to create a bed that promises cloudlike comfort.

179
Replace flannel sheets and wool blankets with pastel sheets and a light coverlet for an easy spring makeover.

A second quilt draped over a wooden rack adds color and coziness on a winter night.

Restful, Refreshing Color

181

Here, black invigorates a gray-blue room and allows cool metals—nickel hardware, an aluminum table, and chrome lamp base—to fit right in. Textiles applied in artful ways soften the look.

182

Dividing a wall horizontally by using two paint colors can create the same visual effect as having expensive chair-rail molding installed.

If the room is sparsely furnished, color will add any needed visual interest. Paint the bed in the same hue as the trim to unite the room's elements into a restful whole.

184

To spruce up a bedroom with minimal effort and expense, paint just one wall with a cheery color. It can be easily changed with the next season.

185

Paint colors can change the apparent size of a room. For a cozy feel, for example, paint the bedroom ceiling the same warm color as the walls. To make a smaller bedroom seem more expansive, paint the ceiling white.

186
Striped or printed wall coverings can be used to visually change the proportions of a room, making a ceiling seem higher or a large space more intimate.

187
Wall coverings can mask surface flaws better than paint and provide better protection in high-traffic areas.

 Creative Touches

188

Repurpose an old barn door uncovered at a salvage warehouse; turn it sideways to make a country-chic headboard.

189

Informal furnishings can bring a country cottage feel to a more formal or urban space.

190

To add volume and visual interest, try partnering a vintage mirror with a trio of vases or other interesting objects. White objects will add space, while colorful objects will brighten a room.

A single floral accent can transform a setting from spare to serene.

192
Wallpapers in vintage designs can be quite pricey. But framing a generous square of a favored pattern achieves a wonderful, decorative effect.

193 Add your own trim—vintage or new—to old or store-bought pillows to give a handcrafted touch to furnishings.

194 Dressed-up journals, cheerful gingham prints, and vintage jewelry boxes can bring fun accents of fresh color into a bedroom.

Children's Rooms

195
A child's room must balance the parent's need for order with the child's need to express his or her personality.

196
Stacked benches and wooden boxes make excellent storage while keeping treasures in plain view.

197
Sturdy furnishings are the rule for a boy's room. Choose solid, functional furniture that your kids are not likely to outgrow.

198

Maps are not only colorful wall art, but also tools for learning geography.

Active children like reminders of their favorite activities in their rooms. A wire basket keeps sports equipment visible but neat. A corkboard wall covering applied floor to ceiling and then framed creates a bulletin board of epic proportions, perfect for pinning up sports-team memorabilia, photos, and maps.

200

In a room that two children share, mixing works better than matching and allows each child to express his or her own tastes and preferences.

201

Utilitarian jars show off small collections well, including marbles, rocks, seashells, or, in this case, PEZ dispensers.

202

A toy ironing board found at a flea market and refurbished with a new cover makes a handy temporary play or storage area.

203
Multifunctional items help keep a room organized by supplying children with adequate storage space and thus, room to play. A reconditioned locker basket chest allows children to have clearly labeled personal storage areas.

204
Bright toys with unique shapes can be used as colorful decorative accents on shelves or in other unexpected places.

205

Quilts tucked at the bottom of beds are perfect for nap time. Choose blankets that are snuggly, durable, fire resistant, and easy to wash.

206

Create a safe haven. A child's quarters should feel happy and familiar.

207

When decorating kids' rooms, get them involved. Ask for their input and take them to the home improvement store to get their reactions and opinions.

208

A good way to ensure that your children will like their bedrooms is to let them help choose the basic color of the walls, and then mix and match the color of their bedspreads and pillows.

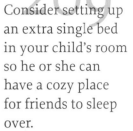

209
Consider setting up an extra single bed in your child's room so he or she can have a cozy place for friends to sleep over.

210
Choose sheets and towels in colors the kids like. Versatile linens can pull a room together with combinations of color and texture.

211
Personalization helps children develop a sense of ownership and responsibility. Using wooden letters from a craft store, stencils, or other materials, help kids make signs identifying their spaces.

212

Neutrals add a soothing quality to a child's room and also act as a unifying element in a space with a lot going on.

213

If a child's room is small, try painting just one wall in a bright color and leaving the others neutral. This technique can go a long way toward brightening a room without making it appear even smaller.

214
Wallpaper is an inexpensive way to decorate your children's rooms with a cheerful, interesting pattern that will help them have sweet dreams at night.

215
Think vertical: bunk beds or trundle beds can double your sleeping capacity without infringing on space.

216
Kids have lots of stuff, and so need lots of places to store and display it. Repurpose antique desks and trunks into kid-friendly organizers of toys, books, and bears.

217
Make the most of wee-sized rooms with storage boxes, cubbyholes, functional furniture, and well-placed hooks and shelves.

218
For younger children, store favorite things in cubbyholes that they can reach.

219
A cozy, under-the-eaves space is perfect for a twin bed. The angled wall also makes an interesting place to pin photos of friends and fun posters.

220
If space permits, create different zones for different activities: the "play zone" can include a table for games and hobbies, while the "study zone" will need to be near outlets for computers and lamps.

Bathrooms

 Traditional country bathrooms are light-filled, airy, and welcoming. Antique claw-foot tubs, simple beveled mirrors, and the colors of the ocean are familiar elements of style in the room we associate with cleansing water, fragrant soap, and fluffy towels. The bathroom is almost like a meditation room, a place where we can either refresh and renew ourselves for the coming day or relax in a hot bubble bath before retiring for the night.

Homeowners suffering sticker shock after inquiring into the cost of new fixtures often write off a bathroom renovation as an impossibly expensive undertaking. It need not be—there are dozens of low-cost ways to give your bathroom an uplifting makeover. Painting, replacing aged faucets, choosing bright towels and bathrugs, and updating window treatments can change a humdrum space into a mermaid's paradise. A few simple accessories will also bring memories of the beach and the sea to your bathtime.

The Essentials: Light and Color

221

Change window treatments and add large mirrors to amplify available natural light.

222 Paint the untiled walls of a bathroom a simple clean color such as lemon or pale blue.

223 Avoid spending money on flashy background materials like handmade tiles. Opt for plain white, creating a neutral canvas for more colorful accessories and linens.

224
Good lighting is essential. Install multiple light sources to allow light to be adjusted for function or mood.

Bring an updated look to a tired, standard tub or basin by installing new faucets.

226

If you have enough space above your sink, hang a large old mirror with a new frame.

227

Vintage lighting can not only provide the traditional look you seek, but can also be less expensive than new reproductions.

228
This fifty-dollar mahogany veneer dresser "with good bones" was converted into a marble-topped double vanity. Look for a similar piece at auctions and flea markets.

229
If you share a bathroom with more than one person, a vanity with lots of drawers gives you more personal storage space.

230 Pressed tin panels painted white offer a period-appropriate alternative to the more usual tiles or beaded board.

231
Staying within a period can strengthen your decorating concept. Here, vintage fabric attached to an early nineteenth-century porcelain sink complements the 1920s cotton curtains acquired at an antique fair.

232
A cast-iron pedestal tub from the early nineteenth-century and an old New England cabinet from a junk shop complete the look.

233
Real stone flooring is expensive, but a similar effect can be achieved with look-alike ceramic tiles, many styles of which are manufactured affordably in Italy.

Reproductions of vintage sinks are now being made by many bathroom fixture companies, but you can save money by spending some time scouring salvage yards for originals.

235
A skylight brightens what might otherwise be a dark and cramped bathroom, part of an attic renovation. The large mirror helps disperse the light.

236
Recycled office and medical furniture such as this sink has become quite popular and provides excellent storage space. It is extremely durable, easily painted for a color change, and typically inexpensive.

237
To cut the time and expense required for tile installation, buy two-inch floor tiles in one-foot square sheets.

238

Creative repurposing is a powerful tool for the decorator on a budget. Here, gym locker baskets are enlisted for bathroom storage.

239 A large galvanized tub can be used as the basin for an old-fashioned sink in a guesthouse bathroom.

240

Why choose between them?
Multiple antique mirrors
can brighten a bathroom.

241

To save space in a narrow bathroom, mount a small pedestal sink in the corner following the angle.

242

Choose a small mirror with an interesting frame to hang in a narrow bathroom, and use a bench or small trunk for toiletries.

243 Small spaces call for cheery colors. Painting a claw-foot tub in the same hue as the walls brightens the whole room.

244 Don't be afraid to go with the color you like, especially when it is mood-enhancing. Yellow trim, bath towels, furnishings, and accessories make this cozy bathroom an inviting place to relax.

Bring the Outdoors Inside

245

Let a jar of ribbons and bottles of lavender- and violet-scented eau de toilette echo the jewel tones of a hydrangea and sedum bouquet.

246

Let the colors of your favorite flowers—hyacinth blue, crimson, or cream—lead the way, then layer on the floral accents.

Relax and enjoy your beautiful bathroom. Pour a relaxing and aromatic bath by letting hot water run over a nosegay of fresh lavender leaves and blossoms.

248

Make a pretty mobile from shells and hang it near a bathroom window.

Decorate window-
sills with seashells
and antique glass
bottles filled with
beach sand.

Overlooked Spaces

 Careful attention to special-purpose spaces—storage areas, mudrooms, home offices, utility rooms, and porches—allows the rest of the rooms of the house to function as they were intended. If the kids can be taught to doff and store coats and boots in the mudroom, for example, there is a better chance that those cast-off items of clothing will not block someone from sitting at the kitchen table. If a home office can be established in a suitable out-of-the-way nook or space, it's less likely that paper and projects will have to be swept off the dining room table when guests are about to arrive. Here is an ample supply of ideas for properly setting up and outfitting your home's special spaces on a budget.

Closets, Drawers, and Storage Secrets

250 As a first step to getting that closet organized, pull everything out and sort honestly and thoughtfully. If you haven't used an item in the last year or more, chances are you never will.

251 An old painted kitchen cupboard makes a perfect place to stack your colorful linens in the bedroom or upstairs hall; it keeps them conveniently visible and saves valuable closet space.

252 Don't forget that items taken to a thrift shop are considered a charitable donation for tax purposes. Be sure to get a receipt.

253 Keep like items together, but things you use fairly often within arm's reach.

254

Old linen cabinets are not hard to find at flea markets. When painted a fresh white, they provide extra storage and country style in a room with limited closet space.

255

A cabinet or armoire with shelves and drawers is priceless. If you have few or small closets, there's an affordable alternative—many budget home-furnishing retailers carry inexpensive cabinets.

256

Display frequently used items that have decorative appeal. Books, candles, flower vases, serving dishes, and, even plates and glassware can become interesting when grouped in small displays.

257

This lovely old card catalogue does duty as a storage area for table linens, napkin rings, candles, and silverware.

258
Antique bandboxes provide elegant and colorful storage.

259
The least expensive way to create more space is to organize clutter and eliminate what you don't need.

260
It's hard to get rid of familiar objects, so start with those you really don't need such as old phone books, games with missing pieces or those your family no longer plays, clothes that don't fit, excess wrapping and packing materials you've been saving (but have too much to ever use up).

261
Hide items that need to be protected or masked from view. Trunks, baskets, file boxes, and plastic containers are all options for hidden storage.

262

Use short bottles to create a kitchen spice drawer, freeing up the taller storage space in your upper cabinets.

263

Make a desk drawer more useful by dividing it into spaces for rubber bands, staples, paper clips, etc. You'll probably discover you have more supplies than you need and can give some away.

264

Add hooks for hanging storage to side walls and a hanging shoe rack to the back of the door.

265 A crate painted white and mounted on wheels makes convenient under-table storage. In the kitchen it is perfect for extra pots and pans or a portable cookbook shelf.

266 Storing loose items in baskets or boxes makes shelves look neater.

267

For whose who crave organization—and most linen closets could use a little more—tack on metal brackets to hold paper labels that can be changed as needed.

268 Cedar closets are wonderful but can lose their aromatic power over time. Sand lightly to restore fragrance and rub in a coat of cedar oil.

269 To brighten a closet, cover tops and fronts of shelves with white, self-adhesive shelf paper, available at craft stores.

270 To dress up the shelves, use double-sided tape to fasten a lace border to the front edge.

Mudrooms

Keep the mudroom organized by providing hooks, baskets, net bags, and surfaces so that everything has a place.

Mudrooms should be tough; beaded board walls, tile floors, and rustic furniture are ideal for taking hard wear.

273

A well-designed mudroom bench not only allows comfortable donning and doffing of footwear, but also provides additional storage.

A durable mudroom floor can be had to suit any budget, from cork and laminates at the low end to ceramic titles and stone at the high end, with good old wood right in the middle.

Home Offices

An empty wall of a great room can be turned into a family work station with storage for all.

276

An unused nook or corner can provide space for a laptop and a writing table.

277

Tucking the home-office equipment into a closet, alcove, or armoire can free a room to function as it was originally intented.

278

When we cannot allocate an entire room for a home office, a curtain covering an alcove space will do just as well.

279
Desks and filing cabinets can be prohibitively expensive, so if you want to get organized on a budget, you'll have to think outside the box.

280
Paint a simple sawhorse table and chair to make a basic but useful computer/office area.

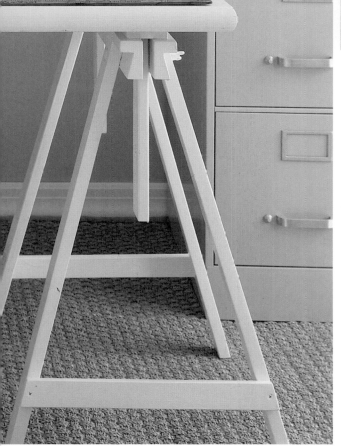

281

A discarded
stationer's card-
display rack here
becomes an office
reminder stand,
while a new role
box holds mail
and bills.

282

An old frame of any kind can be used to make a handy and decorative bulletin board.

283

Repurpose a time-worn muffin pan as a handy drawer organizer.

284
Have a home for everything. Magazine boxes, file cabinets, bookshelves, and storage bins will all help.

285
Use wall space. A bulletin board covered with a pretty floral print will keep letters, notes, and important reminders in plain sight.

286
Use a china or ceramic pitcher for storing colored pencils—it's a practical way to bring brightness into your work space.

287
A painted wicker desk lends country charm to the room in which you've chosen to work.

288 Personalize your space. Find a chair you are comfortable with, both physically and visually. Use vintage curtain tie-back pushpins and intriguing wallpaper samples to make your mark.

289 An inexpensive three-tiered chrome-metal stand makes an excellent organizer for either thin or bulky items.

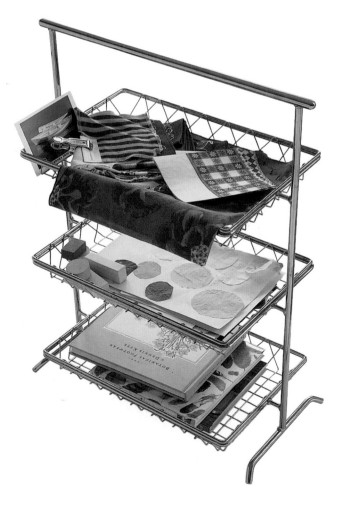

290

Dig your tool carrier out of the garage or basement and repurpose it for organizing basic office supplies.

291

An extra-long pine-plank flea market bench can serve as a magazine rack and fax machine station for a busy at-home worker.

Laundry Rooms

292 Front-loading washers and dryers necessitate stooping to load and unload, but make possible a wide, clean counter-top area in a small laundry space.

293 For a weekend cottage, new combined washer-dryer appliances can be tucked away in closet-sized spaces.

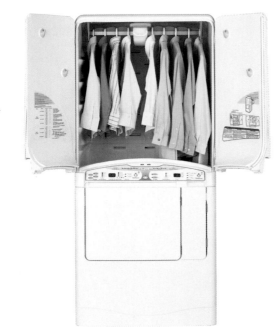

294 Individual, labeled baskets help clean, folded clothes find their way to their rightful owners.

295 Practical storage can still be whimsical and unusual. Clothespin bags from the 1930s and 1940s are colorful, cute, and typically sell for as little as twelve dollars.

296
Under the deep sink is a sizable storage area, which can be made to look neater with the aid of curtains on a rod. Of course, nothing should be placed here that might be a danger to curious kids or pets.

297
An antique dollhouse has a new purpose as storage space for laundry supplies.

Open shelving gives easy access to all your laundry supplies.

Porches

299 Expand your home's living space by thinking of the porch as a true room that just happens to be out-doors.

300 Outfitted with a long, sturdy wooden table and chairs, the porch functions as a dining room.

301 To complete the illusion of an actual room, add a wall mirror reflecting the garden opposite, and a side table that can serve as a buffet or bar.

302
A sheltered porch is an ideal place to set up a potting area; as a less formal room, it's okay if it gets a little dirty, and you have a place to work on rainy days.

303
In creating your porch potting area, have fun with finds from yard sales and furniture that might otherwise be on its way out. Here, a happy marriage of an old table bottom and a separate top makes a charming but sturdy workstation.

304 An attractive, small Victorian table painted with a water-resistant gloss paint adds a grace note to your outdoor room.

305 The addition of a wicker reading lamp and a rack of magazines can make a porch an inviting, calm place to relax and read when the house is full or noisy.

306 Mix and match fabric patterns on cushions and throw pillows. Don't be afraid to have fun with your porch—not everything has to match perfectly.

 # Cellars

307 Improving the cellar for use as a workspace or for storage can take the pressure off upstairs living space. However, you must first assess the conditions, especially whether damp or dry.

308 Consult an expert, in fact several experts, about a cellar that has occasional standing water. Many cellar leaks can be fixed or at least ameliorated with simple, solutions, such as gutter or downspout repair and waterproof patching.

309 You can still use a damp cellar for storage, but consider using stacking plastic boxes and avoid storing fabrics, books, and paper items that are more susceptible to mold.

310

Cellars that are only slightly damp can be improved by running a dehumidifier.

311

Most cellars are darker that they need be. Lighten things up with overhead fluorescent lights with pull switches, easily hung and plugged into existing outlets.

312

A classic country cellar can double as a pantry—store picnic baskets, freshly picked herbs, and farm fresh produce in a cool spot until you are ready to use them.

313

If you have a roomy, dry cellar, use it as a workspace for woodworking, refinishing, or other do-it-yourself projects.

314

If you set it up with adequate lighting, your cellar can be your own private studio for sketching, carpentry, or storing special wine.

315

Consider how you
will be using your
cellar, whether for
work or storage.
This will determine
your requirements
for insulation and
electricity.

Maintaining the Interior and Exterior

 What does maintaining a home involve? We may recall courses in school dubbed "home economics," but those mostly concentrated on ways to provide healthy and delicious meals for the family on a reasonable budget. Maintaining a home economically requires a much wider range of knowledge and skills.

Bringing budgetary common sense to the modern country home involves basic decisions about purchasing an older home as a fixer-upper—an undertaking that seems to have broad appeal in spite of its difficulty. It also involves conserving energy to avoid bills that devour a healthy share of the family income. Maintaining a home is also about upkeep and efforts to preserve and enhance its value, or "curb appeal." It even addresses ways to off-load the "trash and treasures" in your closets and garage—at a tag sale or perhaps an online auction.

❧ Renovating

316 Renovating an old home yourself can be the ultimate project. But to make it a money-saving project you must be honest in assessing what needs to be done, and how much of it you can do yourself.

317 Eliminate guess-work. Get written estimates from several contractors for all improvements needed.

318 When considering purchasing a property for renovation, always have it evaluated by a licensed home inspector.

319 Honestly assess your renovating goals. Will you be using new materials and fixtures or restoring everything to a period, which can be much more costly?

320 Honestly assess your skills. Electrical and plumbing jobs are not the best projects upon which to test your do-it-yourself knowledge.

321 Keep a notebook of all you have done to upgrade your home, including contact information on all workers and suppliers. The information will be handy in case you have to replace or alter something in the future, and the record will enhance the resale value of your property.

322 Prioritize. Knowing what you must have right away (a working bathroom?) and what can be done down the road (painting and wallpapering?) will help you stick to and stretch a budget.

Conserving

323 Uncover sun-warmed windows in winter. On sunny days, south-facing living rooms often stay warm enough to avoid turning up the heat.

324 In summer, shade south-facing windows. Even better, if you have awnings, lower them to block the sun's heat before it reaches your living areas.

325 In winter, set the thermostat back to fifty-five degrees Fahrenheit (newer units do this automatically) while you sleep snuggled under warm blankets. No use heating the whole house all night.

326 "People" heat raises the temperature. When entertaining, guests will be more comfortable, and you'll economize, by turning the thermostat down a few degrees.

327 Use your microwave instead of the gas oven when you can. The energy cost for heating using your microwave is as much as ninety percent less.

328 The next time you buy light bulbs consider fluorescents, now available in many forms to fit incandescent bulb sockets. Fluorescents last ten times longer and use a quarter of the electricity that incandescent bulbs use.

329 Check your home for cold drafts in the winter, which often can be felt around openings to or seams closing off colder spaces, such as electrical outlets and where walls meet floors. Caulk or insulate those openings.

330 In the basement, caulk the joint between the top of the foundation wall and the first wooden member.

331 Weather-strip the cellar door.

332 A wood-burning stove can save on winter heating bills by warming the bedroom or living area while the thermostat is turned down. Many new EPA-approved models burn far more efficiently than antiques.

333 Studies show that more than half of the 75 million single-family homes in America are under-insulated. Adding insulation to the attic, for example, can make a big difference in your heating bill.

334 Deciduous trees planted to the south and southwest of the house can block the sun and cool the house by as much as twenty degrees Fahrenheit, and at no cost. Potted plants on the porch add a cool feel as well.

335 Awnings can reduce solar heat gain by 64 to 77 percent, making them by far the most economical cooling devices available.

336 Replacing outdated appliances with energy-efficient models can provide significant savings in the long run.

337 Other ways to save both your money and the environment: use leftover cooking water to refresh house plants, run the dishwasher only when full, and fix leaky faucets.

338 When choosing new appliances, look for models that are rated highly by the strict Energy Star guidelines of the Environmental Protection Agency and the U. S. Department of Energy. In a recent year these appliances helped save consumers 7 billion dollars, not to mention enough energy to power a million homes.

339 You don't need expensive electric filters to improve the air quality of your home. The first step is as simple as opening windows to get fresh air circulating.

340 Avoid storing unused pesticides in the house, and minimize the use of air fresheners and scented candles, which can cause irritation to the eyes and throat.

341 To inhibit mold growth, eliminate any standing water by cleaning the water pans in air conditioners and refrigerators, and tending to any plumbing leaks, however small.

342 New shower curtains, draperies, and carpeting can give off potentially harmful fumes, so let them air out on a clothesline for a day or two before installation.

343 Look for rugs that bear the Carpet and Rug Industry tag, an industry standard that identifies products meeting low levels of "off gassing."

344 Allergy sufferers should consider living without carpets, which can harbor dust mites, bacteria, and mold.

345 Ordinary potted plants absorb common household gases such as formaldehyde, ammonia, and benzene, thereby improving indoor air quality.

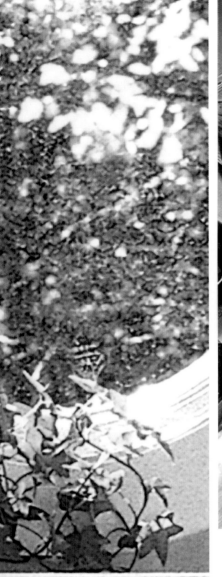

346
Carefully consider storage methods for spices and herbs, which, ounce for ounce, are likely the most expensive foodstuffs in your kitchen. Spices do not "spoil," but can lose flavor and strength over time if not properly stored.

347
After grinding or powdering, spices should be kept in small tin canisters with tight lids, or other containers that block out light as well as seal out air.

349
Whole spices will stay fresher longer than ground spices. Whole spices can be stored in lidded glass jars, which lock in freshness and allow you to keep tabs on supplies.

348
Refrigerate oil-rich seeds, like poppy and sesame, as well as red-colored spices, including red-pepper flakes, paprika, and chili powder.

Selling at Tag Sales and Auctions

350 When it comes time to part with furnishings that just don't fit in any more, or just to clear out clutter, holding a tag sale can be a way to finance, at least partially, your anticipated new look.

351 Share the workload and make your tag sale more exciting by joining with friends who also have items to dispose of.

352 Always check with your local chamber of commerce or town hall to find out about any regulations or needed permits.

353 Spread the word as widely as possible. Local newspaper ads and prominent signs on the day of the sale are most effective.

354 Sort items by category (toys, glass, linens, etc.) or price range ("all items on this table two dollars"). Mark prices clearly and be sure to have plenty of change on hand.

355 You customers may want to bargain, so for items of significant value, have a sense of how low you will be willing to go.

356 On the day of the auction think about whether you really want to attend. If you are disposing of a treasured piece you may decide not to.

357 Any avid collector knows that the way to stretch the buying budget is to sell periodically. The competitive bidding of auctions can often ensure the fairest price for what you wish to dispose of, especially if your item is unusual or rare.

358 Know your items and their value before your sell. Many auction houses offer free appraisals on special days or may be glad to evaluate your item if you make an appointment. For very valuable items, pay for an expert appraisal if necessary.

359 Choose an auction house that regularly deals with items or collections similar to yours. Talk to other customers about their experiences with the company.

360 Serve refreshments at a modest price. This adds to the festive feel of your sale and causes people to linger and keep looking.

361 Be clear on the fees. In most cases you are responsible for delivering the items, shipping, and insurance if required, and even the photography needed for listing in the auction house catalogue. In addition, commission rates vary from between 15 and 25 percent, depending upon the final price and the policy of the auctioneer.

362 If you feel it does not make sense to sell below a certain price, set a "reserve," a minimum price that must be met.

Improvements to the Exterior

363 To set off a house that might otherwise seem too ordinary, paint the fence a bright, cheery color.

364 For a quick exterior fix on a house that is just too plain, add shutters, or paint existing shutters in a complementary, contrasting color. Shutters not only make windows look larger, by framing interior decor they give the home a warmer, more inviting look.

365 Light the way to your home at night with elegant outdoor lighting, now available in inexpensive, install-it-yourself sets.

366 Classic and elegant street numbers make a good first impression.

367

Money was saved on this main-entrance renovation by building over this plain concrete stoop to create a full wooden patio area.

368

A fresh coat of paint is the best way to perk up a tired-looking home.

369

Cleaning house siding with a pressure washer will remove dirt that can pit the surface over time.

Accesorize a dull exterior with texture and color. Window boxes with bright flowers and inexpensive plastic shutters work wonders.

371

A picket fence can dramatically frame and call attention to your home.

372

Replacing square front-porch supports with heavier columns is an inexpensive way to make a home appear more solid and substantial.

373

Reproduction wooden trim can be used to restore the traditional details that many homes built more recently lack.

374

Wooden shutters, usually no longer functional, can make windows appear bigger and provide the opportunity to add another color to accent your trim.

375 Gravel drives and paths present a more natural and appealing surface, and can cost half as much as conventional paving.

376

Gravel comes in a wide range of colors, including warm earth tones, that can set off your country home and its plantings dramatically.

377

To install a proper gravel drive or walk, the base should be excavated to a depth of least a foot and then compacted. Rough debris on the bottom is followed by a layer of crushed stone and finally, two or three inches of river-washed gravel.

378 The secret to keeping gravel in place is to install borders of larger stones, cobbles, or bricks.

379 Upkeep of gravel areas is often thought to be onerous. In fact, weeding in low traffic areas and raking a few times each year are all that is required.

Patios, Decks, and Outdoor Rooms

380 Lay a small brick patio as a first step in creating an outdoor room; using brick, it is easy to get professional results on a do-it-yourself budget.

381 Contact local suppliers, who will show you patterns and designs, and deliver the materials you need: brick, sandstone edging, crushed limestone, and sand.

382 A twelve- by fifteen-foot rectangle is a manageable weekend project and suitable for containing such flea market finds as a rustic table for potting or dining, comfortable seating, and a variety of planted decorative pots and urns.

383
The most common construction material for decks is pressure-treated wood, which is inexpensive and long-lasting. However, it can splinter and presents waste-disposal problems, so shopping around is worthwhile.

384
A deck too high and "out there" will expose users to sun and elements that may make it uninhabitable. If a steep slope does not permit a terrace, of course, a deck may be the only alternative.

385
While adding a deck can provide more outdoor living space economically, you must carefully consider design, placement, and materials.

386

If the area is level, you might consider instead a terrace with a protective awning or pergola structure overhead. Decks require building permits whereas terraces generally do not.

387

Natural cedar resists rot, but is soft and wears readily, while fir must be treated periodically with preservatives. Consider new varieties of plastic lumber, which have the look and feel of wood. They cost more initially, but they will last indefinitely without much maintenance.

Caring and Conserving

 From the budget point of view, caring for what you own is perhaps second in importance only to the cost of acquisition. If you spend anything at all on an item and do not care for it properly, chances are that your expenditure will be wasted; conversely, if you understand general principles of repairing and conserving, you can probably get a bargain on valuable items overlooked by those who don't have your knowledge.

Learning how to recane chairs, rewire lamps, or refinish wooden furniture all allow you to turn flea market bargains into useful and valuable items, which you can keep in your home or even resell. In this chapter are some basic tips for conserving and preserving that require no special skills or techniques—only a desire to keep and appreciate what you have already collected.

❦ Linens

388 After going to the trouble and expense of collecting those antique linens, proper care will ensure that they last indefinitely, even with regular use.

389 Correct storage prevents linens from yellowing and streaking. Wrap treasured heirloom textiles in acid-free paper, then place them in a container lined with unbleached muslin.

390 Inspect and refold linens you use rarely to prevent them from becoming musty or wrinkled from sitting in your linen closet.

391 Treat stains as swiftly as possible before they set. Rinse coffee spills with boiling water before laundering; rub salt into fruit stains, soak in cold water, then cold wash.

392 Normally, warm-water washing with liquid soap or gentle detergent cleans linens most effectively.

393
Non-chlorine bleach may work to whiten linens yellowed by age or improper storage.

394
To ensure a crisp finish it is best to iron durable linens when damp, stretching each piece to its full shape.

395
Wash non-vintage, store-bought linens once a week in the hottest water available and encase mattresses and pillows in zippered dust-proof covers. Vacuum mattresses and rotate them twice a year.

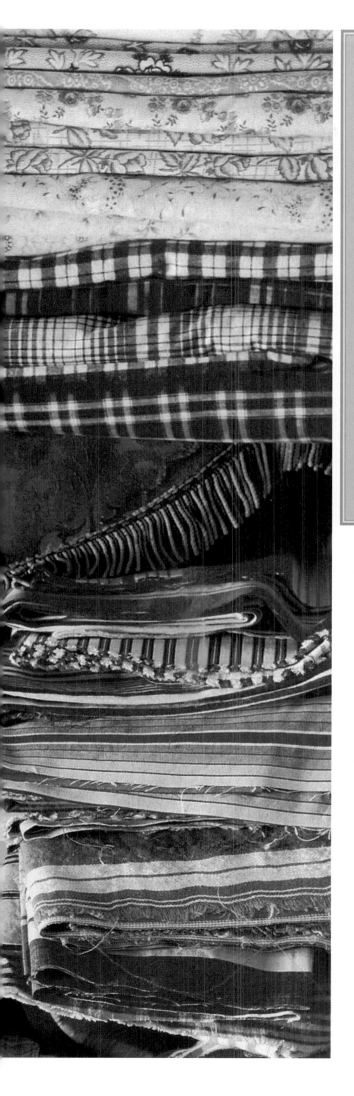

❧ Environment-Friendly Products

396

For wood floors sealed with polyurethane, mop with a mixture of one gallon of warm water and a cup of white vinegar.

397

To freshen carpets and neutralize odors, liberally sprinkle with baking soda, let stand overnight, then vacuum.

398

Use a paste made of lemon juice and baking soda to scrub away mildew on shower tiles and plastic shower curtain liners.

399

You can be environmentally sensitive and save money at the same time by using natural products for cleaning. Mildly abrasive baking soda cleans bathtubs, kitchen sinks, and grimy pots and pans

Upholstery

400 Reupholstering is the most expensive method of refurbishing a chair or sofa, suitable for a cherished heirloom or a quality piece with a sturdy frame.

401 Before deciding on any furniture refurbishing plan, carefully assess the room and the activities that take place there. You may not want to pay for reupholstering a couch favored by pets and snacking kids watching TV.

402
Vacuum upholstery regularly using the appropriate attachment of your vacuum cleaner and use the crevice-cleaning attachment to get into the seams. Rotate sofa cushions.

403
Be sure to carry swatches of draperies, paint colors, or carpeting to the store when researching fabric choices. And bring some fabric samples home to contemplate for a while before deciding.

404

Custom slipcovers can approximate reupholstering for far less money. And if someone is dispatched to your home to take measurements, you will not have to do without your furniture for several weeks.

405

Ready-made slipcovers are ideal for households with young children or pets, as they are easily removed for washing.

406
Vacuuming window treatments means a longer time between washing or expensive dry cleaning.

407
Properly cleaning and caring for upholstery, drapes and bedding can prolong their life and brighten a dull-looking room.

Antique Board Games

408 Preserve and protect your collection of antique board games (or bandboxes or other early products incorporating printed paper or wood) by cleaning only very cautiously. Gently rub the soiled surface using a damp cloth and mild, non-abrasive detergent, taking care not to saturate the surface.

409 Keep your collection out of direct sunlight, which can quickly dull colors. If you display your collection at home or in the office, rotate and rearrange items regularly.

410
If you frame a board game or other item, consider acrylic sheets with a layer of UV protection.

411
Proper storage is essential. Avoid temperature extremes, and the damp and mildew of basements. Avoid using rubber bands and paper clips, which can cause damage over time, and do not stack items too deeply.

412
Never make repairs using ordinary adhesive tape, which is typically highly acidic and will deteriorate paper and cardboard with time. Use archival tape instead, available at framing and stationer's shops.

Special Photographs

413 Photos that are seldom viewed should be stored laid flat in sturdy archival boxes; for extra protection, layer acid-free tissue or museum-quality matte board between the images.

414 Vintage photographs and cherished family portraits perfectly suit the needs of budget-minded decorators. However, care in handling and storage is essential to preserving your valuable images.

Once or twice a year, rotate
framed photographs that
are exposed to sunlight.

416

Use today's inexpensive scanning and printing technology to create duplicates for display where sunlight is unavoidable, storing originals carefully away.

417

Photographs not framed on walls can be displayed in albums with acid-free pages and "photo corners" that hold images without adhesives.

418
Exposure to direct sunlight is the greatest threat to photographs. Frame your photographs under glass or Plexiglas that has a layer of UV for protection.

419
Be aware that many albums produced through the 1960s were made with highly acidic paper, and photos stored in them should be moved.

China and Ceramics

420
A budget approach to collecting and decorating involves conserving. Follow these guidelines to keep your antique and cherished ceramic pieces safe and in the best possible condition.

421
Always use both hands and a secure grip when moving ceramics. Grasp the body rather than handles or finials, which are the weakest parts.

422
When stacking, place heavier pieces on the bottom and lighter ones on the top.

423

A cushioning device like a square of cotton flannel should be placed between pieces when stacking and storing valuable sets.

424

To avoid chipping, make sure any wall mounting holds your plate or platter securely without exerting too much pressure on the edges.

425

Unless a glazed surface is extremely worn, accumulated dirt and grime can be removed with a soft brush or a gently lightly dampened cotton flannel cloth, using either water alone or a solution containing a few drops of mild dish washing detergent.

426

Always wash pieces one at a time and avoid extreme fluctuations in water temperature. If chips or cracks need repair, consult a professional conservator.

Vintage Ornaments

427 To preserve and protect those treasured holiday ornaments you have collected over the years, take some care in packing and storing. Use a rigid container with adjustable compartments so items cannot knock against each other.

428
Wrap ornaments in acid-free tissue or 100-percent cotton fabric. Avoid using plastic, which retains moisture and breaks down over time, and especially bubble-wrap, which contains gases that may leak and cause discoloration.

429
An ideal location for storage is a closet off the living area of the house. Most attics and garages have temperature fluctuations that are too great, and most basements are too damp.

Sprucing up Outdoor Chairs

430 Get your outdoor furniture ready for another season on the porch or in the garden.

431 Use a vacuum cleaner to remove loose dust and dirt, then wash with scrub brush and soap suds to loosen and remove grime

432 Rinse with a garden hose and dry in the sun. Spray on a thin coat of lacquer to protect any worn surfaces.

433
Your outdoor canvas furniture will last longer if you carefully vacuum surface dirt with a low-suction machine.

434
Musty odors resulting from prolonged storing should dissipate naturally by airing. Again, careful vacuuming will speed up the process.

435 Unify a set of mismatched kitchen chairs with a quick makeover. Start with flea-market finds that have seats that pop off with a few screws or bolts.

436 Remove the seats from the chairs, sand chairs lightly, and wipe clean. Apply a cost of primer and let dry. Follow-up with two coats of interior paint in a color you love.

437 Discard the old seat fabric and foam pad. Secure new foam, cut to size, with double-sided tape. Flip over and place on your new fabric; then pull smooth and staple in place.

Fences

The easiest way to dress up a shabby-looking picket fence is to repaint it. A compressed-air paint sprayer can be rented from a local home improvement center.

Painting your picket fence regularly will add many years to its life.

439

440 If you opt for painting by hand, use a roller on the front of the pickets to save time then use a brush on the sides and back.

441 Whether you spray or use a brush, be sure to use a latex-based, rather than oil-based, paint. Latex paint will allow the wood to expand and contract without cracking.

Collecting on a Budget

 Wouldn't your top kitchen shelf look striking arrayed with a collection of pottery in bright and complementary shades? Wouldn't the breakfast table be more fun with juice glasses sporting bold stripes placed on a '50s tablecloth featuring a road map of Florida? And wouldn't the bedroom feel cozier with some vintage quilts piled on a rustic blanket chest at the end of the bed? Such decorative touches are not expensive; they are waiting for you at your local flea markets and antique fairs. It's up to you to imagine what you need and to creatively use what is being offered.

Collecting and displaying objects in groups according to form, function, medium, or color helps to create a sense of cohesiveness. Collect the items you love and play with them until you find a look that suits your fancy. The art of collection and display helps us to communicate with others about who we are.

Smart Strategies

Develop an eye. Begin by looking at the best examples of whatever it is you're collecting and use those as a standard for judging other objects.

Arm yourself with expertise. Read auction catalogues, books, and trade publications; visit museums, historical societies, specialty shops, and the homes of fellow collectors.

144 Don't buy if the object is investment only. Good antiques will hold their value over time, but you may not be able to get top dollar, or your money back, if you decide to sell because you've tired of them.

145 Cultivate the best tools for the collector—common sense and a well-trained eye.

446 Buy because you love what you're collecting and want to live with the items.

447 Follow the dealers— they know the best antique shows—but get there as early as they do for the best selection.

448 In the end, always buy the item that promises to bring you the most pleasure and buy the best example of its kind that your budget will allow.

449
Don't be afraid to ask a dealer as many questions as you like, and ask if the dealer can "do any better" on the price.

450
Above all, don't collect something just because it is deemed "hot." Collecting fads come and go and you will likely be paying top price for those items.

Buying at Flea Markets and Auctions

451 Flea markets are the budget decorator's mall. Here is where you will find the furnishings you need and exciting items to add to your collections, as well as ideas and inspiration.

452 Get there early. Dealers looking to stock their shops swoop in early and grab the most exciting treasures; be sure to be there with them.

453
Wear comfortable shoes and casual clothes, carry a light tote bag, and bring sunglasses and sunscreen. Bring a tape measure, and a notebook and pen for jotting down contacts and ideas.

454
If you are contemplating a purchase of any size, throw some old blankets in the car for wrapping just in case.

455

Ask questions. Dealers should be able to tell you something about any item. But be skeptical as well; sometimes information comes second- or third-hand and can be unreliable.

456

Arm yourself with your own knowledge and experience. In the end, you are your own most reliable authority.

457
Common sense can help you sort real from reproduction. Look for wear consistent with use. Be observant: a popular reproduction will often be displayed at more than one booth.

458
Imagine how an item will look in your home. Flea markets can present a dazzling array of colors and patterns. Pull the item out, place it against a neutral background if possible, then step back and contemplate.

459
Always bargain. Most dealers expect to come down to a "best price." And always carry cash, the payment of choice.

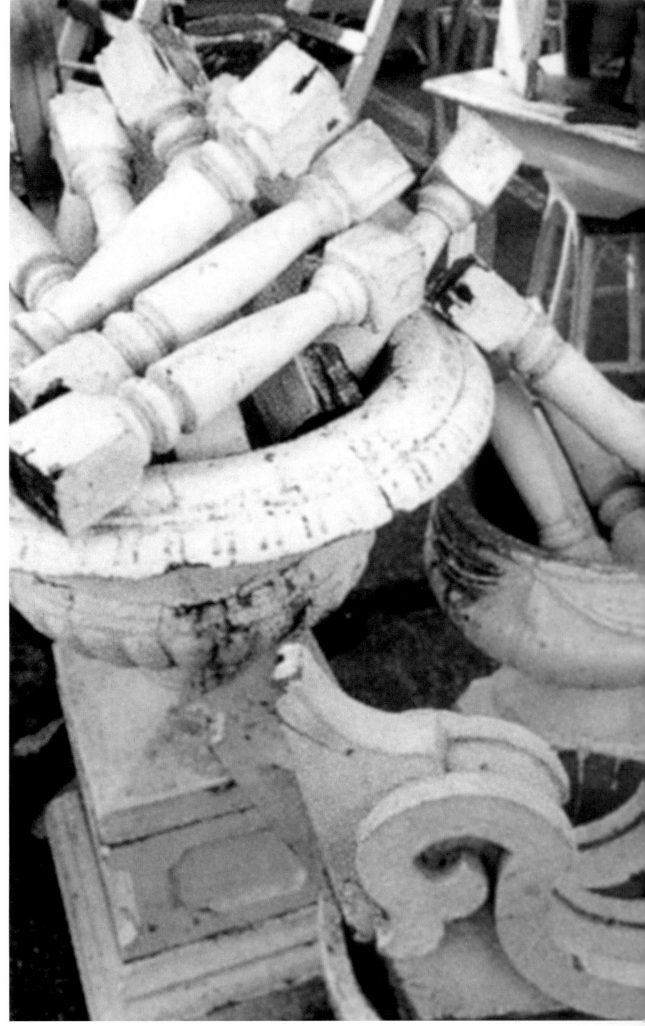

460

Country auctions can be places to find bargains on everything from household appliances and antique furniture to farm equipment and family cars. But you have to follow a few simple rules.

461

Arrive early on the day of the auction, to give you ample time to look over the offerings, to register and get your bidding paddle, and to find out about payment methods, which can vary from auction to auction.

462 Most auction companies adhere to a strict "as is" policy, so inspect items closely before the sale begins. Bring a tape measure and a magnifying glass and whatever other tools you need to assess whether the item is right for you.

463 Determine in advance the top prices you will pay for the items you are interested in and stick to your decisions.

464 When bidding starts, maintain eye contact with the auctioneer to let him know of your continued interest. Concentrate on the numbers during the auctioneer's chant.

465 Make a clear gesture with your paddle to assent to a higher bid and don't be afraid (as many are) that the auctioneer will misinterpret some small movement as a bid.

❧ Buying Online

466
Modern technology has come to the aid of the budget decorator in the form of online auctions. They are a good place to look for those items you collect and good bargains are possible.

467
Nearly 50 million people are registered eBay users, buying and selling almost every conceivable item.

468
Don't skimp on shipping insurance, especially if an item is breakable or costly.

469
Resist paying too much—there's always tomorrow!

470
Online auctions are also a way to clear out an item or collection that no longer fits with your scheme or space.

471
The Internet is an amazing resource, not just for auctions but for information. Find others interested in collecting what you do by going to www.collectors.org.

472
If you're bidding on something you really want, stay on top of the auction's progress until the very end, as last minute bids are common. Remember auctions finish on Pacific Standard Time.

473
If the price is right, take a risk—chances are you'll be pleasantly surprised.

What to Collect

474 Liberate your collecting passion by thinking of broader categories rather than identical matches.

475 Try forming a collection based on function and format, such as a handsome group of engraved silver napkin rings.

Forget about design and go for color and shape: none of these brown-and-white transfer-printed bowls, cups, or plates is an identical match.

477

Set an interesting table by using silverware of various designs and monograms.

478

Serve cordials in antique cordial glasses showing a broad range of styles and patterns.

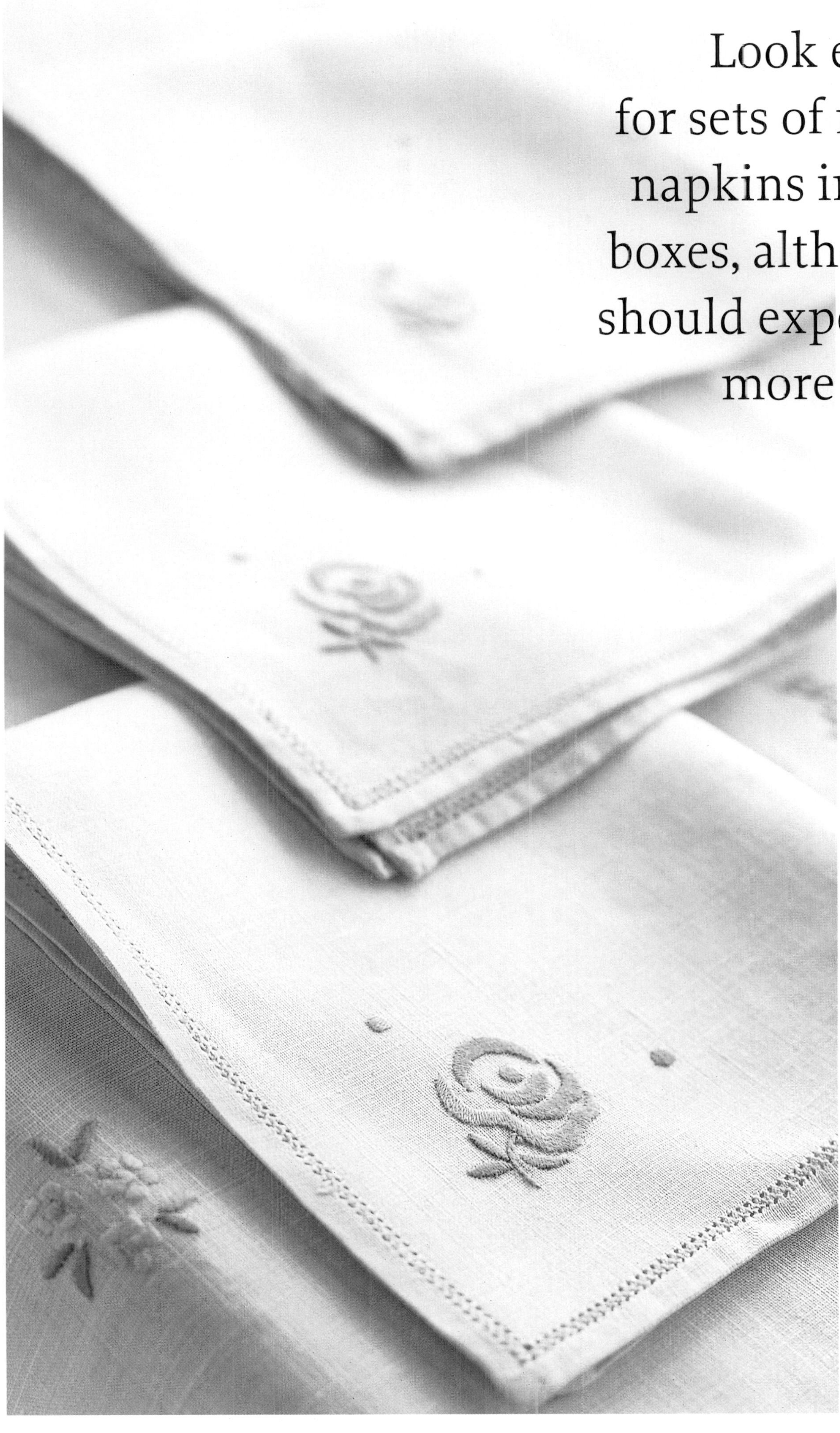

479

Look especially for sets of matching napkins in original boxes, although you should expect to pay more for these.

480

Vintage tablecloths are not only collectibles that you can use, they also convey a sense of hearth and home.

Bold patterns from the 50s and 60s add fun and color to today's table, typically at less than the cost of a new tablecloth. Look for fruits and flowers and regional designs, such as local maps.

482

Look for antique silver at local auctions or flea markets, where it is often available for a fraction of the cost of new silver or even stainless steel (even though old pieces often surpass the new in weight and workmanship).

483

Remember that silver plate consists of a base metal with a coating of silver, whereas sterling is nearly pure silver through and through. Although the former is more affordable, it is susceptible to wear. Both types have lovely patterns and designs.

484

Silver is a soft metal and can easily be scratched or corroded. When using commercial cleaning products, follow directions carefully and remove all residue by washing using a few drops of mild detergent.

485

Collect various serving utensils and display in a complementary piece of glassware.

486

Although antique silver can be a good investment, experts recommend that you buy only what you like and will actually use.

487 Monogrammed linens have become a valued collectible, yet still can be found at estate and tag sales. But to get a bargain, you have to know what to look for.

488 Pieces embroidered with red-colored thread, popular from the late 1800s to the 1920s, are highly desirable and decorative. They were known as "red-work" or "Turkey red," as their red color resembled that of Turkish carpets.

489
Napkin sets like these c. 1900 lace-edge examples will add a nice touch to any table. The more .matching pieces the more valuable the set.

490
Besides an embroidered monogram, look for twisted threads—called "faggoting"—joining borders, as well as scalloped edges.

491
Note the size and intricacy of the lettering. Collectors and decorators today care little for whose monogram is displayed, as long as the workmanship and design are of high quality.

492
Adirondack chairs are a country classic for good reason. They are wonderfully comfortable, look well in the garden, and can withstand the elements for many seasons.

493
Although vintage Adirondack chairs are getting harder to find—going for $75 to $125 at flea markets—new chairs can often be purchased from local woodworkers for as little as $50.

494
Although you will pay a bit more for chairs made of white cedar (rather than pine), these can stay out in the garden year after year with no maintenance.

Decorating for Festive Occasions

In the country, so much more than in the city, the changes of the season order our lives and dictate our activities. They seem to naturally schedule our celebrations, as well, in a progression that stretches from the first inklings of spring's arrival to the holidays that mark the winter solstice.

Along the way, Memorial Day marks the beginning of our "real" summer, the time during which we conspire to live more outdoors than in. The Fourth of July holiday marks high summer, while Labor Day brings the hint of impending autumn and a return to work-day schedules.

Of course we enjoy the seasons in equal measure, but it is the end of summer, even more than New Year's Eve, that for most of us truly marks a passing year. Fall brings us harvest festivals and Thanksgiving and delivers us gently into another winter.

Each of these important dates and seasons we mark with rituals—preparation of special foods, specific activities, and displays of symbols, whether crafted or store-bought, which we share and enjoy in a renewal of our common humanity. In this chapter we offer some budget tips for making those special occasions more special.

495 For easy holiday decorating, first decide on a theme. A favorite color, collectible, or holiday icon will help you focus and decide on everything from invitations to decorations to desserts.

496 Plan ahead—way ahead. You don't want to be searching for the perfect tablecloth on the busiest shopping day of the year.

497 Light up the room. Candles set the mood and create a festive ambiance.

498
Engage the senses. Think about what your guests will be touching, hearing, smelling, and tasting during any get-together. The scent of spiced cider and the crackling of a fire can make an ordinary holiday gathering extraordinary.

499
Bring out the heirlooms—your mother's china, your grandmother's tablecloths, your wedding silver. It should be a special occasion.

500
Bring the outside in with evergreens, twigs, leaves, pine cones, and homemade wreaths. They also help fill your home with wonderful fragrances.

501
A collection of seasonal glassware can become a relatively inexpensive, simple holiday decoration. In the 1950s, more than a dozen makers of peanut butter sold their product in glasses with holiday themes; you can still find them at flea markets for about eight to ten dollars apiece.

502
Use objects you already own in innovative ways. Drape a table with a hand-sewn quilt instead of a tablecloth, cover a chair with a soft blanket, fill a candy bowl with dried autumn leaves and pine cones.

503
Send small gifts home with your guests. Wrap small boxes in pretty gift paper and place at table settings. Inside place lyrics to a particularly meaningful holiday song or poem, tiny chocolates, or personal words from you to them for the holidays.

504 Collect vintage ornaments whenever you see them at estate and tag sales. Even those lacking the parts to clip to the tree can be used for table displays.

505 New ornaments can emulate the look of old by mixing colors and sizes. Fill the gaps by draping vintage blown-glass garlands.

506
Dress the house with natural garlands and wreaths made from boughs and berries collected from your property and joined with garden wire.

507

For a fuller look, choose a tree that is slightly too tall for the room and trim the top branches to fit.

508

Choosing that special tree from a local farm is a fun winter activity. And the tree will not only be less expensive, it will be fresher and last longer.

Valentine's Day: Decorating with Heart

509

Fashion a gift of roses into a floral wreath. Bend a coat hanger into a heart-shaped frame and weave jasmine or grapevine around it. Attach dried rosebuds with florist's wire and add a ribbon.

510

Remember, the hearts and flowers of Valentine's day can be artfully reinvented for any romantic occasion.

511

Frame fabric hearts and decorate with vintage buttons.

Personalize a gift wrapped in plain white paper by adding a small bouquet of roses and a vintage beaded flower.

May Day: Celebrating Spring

513

Host a gardening party to bring together your plant-loving friends. Perennials are the best plants to work with as they will reseed in their new surroundings.

514

Be prepared with a large work surface, fiber pots, potting soil, plant tags, and watering cans.

515
Hold your party several weeks before the season's optimal planting time. Invite your guests to transplant seedlings you have grown on soil covered trays, either indoors or in a cold frame.

516
Guests can take potted seedlings home or return them to the cold frame to be picked up several weeks later when they are ready for planting.

517
Not only do you and your gardening friends get to enjoy the full cycle of a plant's life, but plants grown from seeds are much less expensive than nursery stock.

Fourth of July Parties

518 Show your colors. Decorating for the Fourth of July can be as easy and inexpensive as hanging colorful flags or bunting.

519 Remember that red, white, and blue creates an instant focal point. Be sure to hang your flag where you want the eye to be drawn, to show off a special feature of your home, for example.

520 Bunting can easily be draped by first installing screw eyes and then creating the folds with loops of steel wire.

521

Reinforce your patriotic color scheme with flowers and table settings of red, white, and blue.

522

Remember that your national colors are appropriate all summer long.

Fall Colors—Indoors and Out

523 Get the most out of your summer gardening efforts and extend the season with a fall garden party.

524 Let Mother Nature dictate colors and decor. Snip end-of-summer favorites like baby cabbages and tuck them into clay pots for pretty, natural place settings. Let guests take the potted plants home as colorful reminders of a fun-filled visit.

525 Garden pails and buckets painted in bright shades of red, green, white, and blue provide punchy counterpoints to the various colors of the garden that fill them.

526

Forget paper plates—
for elegant economy,
serve outdoors from a
basketful of assorted
vintage chinaware
collected at tag sales.

527
Gourds can be bored straight through to make a seasonal embellishments for candlesticks.

A plant stand can become a focal point on a buffet table. Use some plants, of course, but add small stacks of plates, a teapot, and other whimsical elements.

Halloween Parties

529

For a Halloween table, avoid pricey plastic decorations. Make a centerpiece out of a spooky branch.

530

Carve a pumpkin and place it on a cake plate, and light it with a votive candle.

531

Fill a compote with candy corn.

532 Turn to nature for colorful autumn leaves and gourds to decorate your table.

533

Use hollowed out apples as cider cups.

534

Combine floating votives and apples in a bucket of water.

535

With a bit of imagi-nation and very little money, you can transform ordi-nary materials into a Halloween party for you and the kids to remember. Try a spooky medieval theme.

536

Shape a sorcerer's hat by stuffing fabric into the rolled band of a fleecy cap.

537

Add an inexpensive old brooch to bring sparkle to a queen's felt medallion.

Larger gourds can also be used with votive candles that cast a glow through artistically carved designs.

539

Apply beaded collars and appliqués salvaged from cast-off clothing to dress up simply crafted capes, robes, and tunics.

540

Use winter squash, second-hand draperies, and candlelight to set the stage for a royal banquet.

Supplement classic treats—like pumpkin seeds, candy corn, gold-foil-wrapped chocolate coins, and cider—with party-themed popcorn balls studded with gem-like dried fruits and sugar cookies in mythical motifs from castles and crowns to dragons and daggers.

Thanksgiving

542

When setting a fall or Thanksgiving table, take a cue from nature and use the season's vibrant colors as a backdrop.

543
Create a dramatic centerpiece by stacking cake stands of different colors and decorating each tier with fruits and flowers.

544
Let kumquats dance along pears; wild berries punctuate yellow roses; green grapes mingle with figs.

545
Keep the individual blooms in your centerpiece fresh by attaching water vials to stems.

546 Use a uniting color—here purple transferware and napkins—to complement the oranges and ambers of your fall table.

547 Decide on the primary colors of your bouquets—here orange and yellow—and group each bunch with graduating shades, ranging from pale to deep.

Gardens

 When you step into a well-designed garden, something just feels right. There's a sense of pleasure, of comfort, and of being at home. While it's tempting to think that this sensation arises from a connection with nature, your reaction is really the result of considerable human contrivance, the product of a series of principles that operate behind the scenes of all well-planned landscapes.

Of the many design considerations at work, perhaps the most important is refining that the various elements of your landscape work together to connect your garden to the house stylistically. Remember, your house is the most important part of your garden (the landscape was, most likely, planned around your dwelling, not the other way around), and without a cohesive style that complements the architectural design, even the costliest and most finely wrought landscapes will fail to satisfy.

Whether you're interested in quickly improving the appearance of your home, increasing your property's value, or merely enhancing the streetscape you see daily, there is no more effective way to go about it than replacing that dreary foundation planting and transforming your yard or garden into a friendly, inviting, green space.

Do-It-Yourself Garden Design

548
Professional garden design can be a costly service. However, by following a few basic guidelines and using common sense you can get very pleasing results.

549
Think before you plant. What overall style are you most comfortable with—formal, semi-formal, totally natural? Visit established gardens in your area to confirm your decision and to get ideas about how to achieve your goals.

550
"Frame" your garden by establishing its boundaries with taller plantings. Any landscape, no matter what size, needs definition to be visually effective.

Your taller framing shrubs can be used to block neighboring structures or unsightly elements. However, they can be used as well to frame a pleasant distant prospect, even one beyond your property.

Create interior divisions. Think of your garden area as a house with rooms that have various functions, one perhaps utilitarian, for growing herbs and vegetables, another filled with pleasant flowers and comfortable seating.

553 Choose native species. Preselected by nature for your area, these plants are hardier, require less water, and typically are cheaper than non-native species.

554 Know when enough is enough. A landscape too divided will cease to function as a cohesive whole. Leave an outlying open space alone, for example, to provide a dramatic backdrop to a series of more intimate garden spaces arranged around the house.

555 Avoid dull row planting. Try deep beds—perhaps 10 to 15 feet—with taller plants in the rear, graduating to smaller specimens at the front. Plant in combinations of threes, fives, and sevens, with an occasional single variety for accent.

556

The goal of your front-yard plantings should be to enhance, not to hide, your home. Pay attention to information on dimensions mature plants will reach.

557

Avoid the suburban look of evergreens only. Create a mixed planting of year-round interest that includes deciduous material as well as evergreens.

Planning Small Gardens

558 Large gardens are actually easier to plan, as there's room for the variety of plantings and a place to hide what you don't want to see—like the compost heap. Small gardens are a challenge that can be overcome by following some simple rules.

559 Supply a focal point. The small garden needs something that draws the eye into the space and allows the mind to make immediate sense of it. A seating area, a birdbath, or an arbor are all possibilities.

560 Plant to scale. Select perennials, shrubs and tress that will not outgrow the site.

561

A small garden can also be made to look larger by planting one or more dwarf trees.

562

Give the garden a unified style. Think of it as an exterior room, with walls (hedges), entrances (gates) and windows (views) that call for a sense of cohesiveness to pull them together.

563

To make a small garden seem larger, create a distinct visual line, using a path or hedge, across the longest available axis.

Boundaries: Fences and Hedges

564

Fencing can define a space, keep critters out of a garden, or block unsightly views. Keep your goals in mind when considering both initial and maintenance costs of the fencing you buy.

565

Rustic fences made from split rail or branches are typically decorative, enhancing rather than blocking views. They can be costly but are usually left to age naturally, requiring little or no maintenance.

566

The standard white picket fence is a favorite, and comes in inexpensive pre-fabricated sections. However, it must be painted initially and periodically there-after.

567
Inexpensive vinyl fencing is popular where ease of maintenance is paramount. It will likely last for 20 to 30 years with no attention, although power washing periodically is recommended.

568
Whatever style fencing you choose to buy, it is wise to discuss your plans with an adjacent neighbor.

569
A high, open plank and board fencing discourages trespassers while letting in sunlight and breezes and allowing vines to climb.

570
In these days of smaller plots for suburban homes, consider planting hedges rather than using fencing to block a neighboring house or unsightly view.

571
A tall hedge can delineate a restful and private garden space.

572
When purchasing hedge plants, pay careful attention to the width and height of the mature plant; otherwise, you may be pruning more often than you planned.

Hedges can also provide a green backdrop to set off more colorful plants in front of them.

Planting Grass and Ivy

574 Tired of the time and expense needed to maintain a large lawn? Consider adding border planting to reduce your lawn's area.

575 If any section of your property is more than 60 percent grass, consider returning a portion of it to meadow, which only has to be cut once a year.

576 For a healthier lawn, sharpen your mower's blades regularly and raise the cutting height as the summer heats up. These simple steps can often eliminate the need for expensive and environmentally unfriendly fertilizers and pesticides.

577

Ivy in the garden and in the house is a green delight. It roots easily from cuttings placed in water, so there is no need to buy it from the nursery.

578

A vigorous climber, ivy has long been used to lend color and life to walls and fences.

Ivy takes naturally to topiary frames of all shapes; for quickest results, use small-leafed varieties and keep the leaves pruned close to the frame.

Kitchen Gardens

From a small space of available lawn, create a small kitchen garden for growing the fresh herbs you love.

581

Choose a spot that has full sun, and is as close to the house as possible, so you don't have to lug your produce too far.

582
Our frugal grand-
parents would
never have thought
of paying for what
they could grow
themselves. A small
kitchen garden can
not only trim the
food budget, but can
provide hours of
gardening pleasure.

583
It is wonderful to be
able to step out to
snip some fresh
herbs whenever you
need them.

584
Even a small garden
takes work weeding
and cultivating, so
be careful not to go
overboard. For
beginners, a twenty-
by twenty-foot plot
is plenty.

585
Chives, red leaf let-
tuce, and purple
cabbage are all
hardy and easy to
grow, and taste better
fresh from your
garden than store
bought.

586
Test your soil to find out what nutrients it needs; you can do this yourself using a kit from a local garden shop.

587
Beds narrow enough to reach across separated by paths are easiest to work with.

588
Grow what you enjoy eating and can use completely. A few zucchini plants produce a lot of squash.

589
Add a few annual flowers for cutting, so you can enhance the look of your table as well as the taste of your food.

590
Rather than pay
$2.99 a pound for
tomatoes, get the
family involved in
the fun of growing
your own.

591
Ask your garden
shop about flavor-
producing trace
minerals, such as
rock dust or kelp
foliar spray.

592
Plant tomatoes in
your sunniest
spot—they need at
least eight hours of
sun a day to develop
their fullest flavor.

593
Fertilize with
compost or rotted
manure before
planting, and
improve yields and
flavor by applying
mulch.

594

Cage plants or tie up vines so that the fruit doesn't drag on the ground.

595

Plant several varieties of tomatoes: cherries for salads, beefsteaks for slicing and sandwiches, plums for making sauces.

596

You needn't go to the trouble of canning if you plan to use your crop up over the next winter. Simply chop, drain, and seed large tomatoes, make sauces of the plum tomatoes, and freeze in plastic bags.

597
Most herb flowers taste like a delicate version of the herb itself; add them whenever a soupçon of herbal flavor is required.

598
Do your research before you harvest, as some species are poisonous.

599
Flower petals can be added to almost any recipe imaginable. Rose, nasturtiums, and chive blossoms make wonderful flavored butters.

600

Get more out of your garden. Those nasturtiums and marigolds not only look pretty, they are edible and can make tasty and colorful additions to your salads.

601

Sprinkle petals over roasts or grilled fish, add them into sauces, or float them in a pot of tea.

602

Don't spray edible flowers with any form of pesticide; they are destined for your plate, not a vase.

603
You don't need an expensive greenhouse to grow spectacular flowers and herbs indoors in winter. But you do have to be realistic when assessing conditions of sunlight and humidity.

604
Six or more hours is considered full sun; you may want to consider incandescent or fluorescent grow lights if natural light is inadequate.

605
Many plants require daily fluctuations in temperature of from 8 to 10 degrees. You can test whether your window area meets this requirement by purchasing a handy "minimum/ maximum thermometer," available at your local hardware store.

606

Make your garden more productive. Ornamental landscapes can easily produce useful and economical fruits, vegetables, and herbs with just some simple changes.

607

Grow only what you like to eat. Don't think that your garden needs to be "nutritionally balanced," just plant your favorites.

Grow what is expensive at the market. Enjoy saving money while you harvest fresher fruits and veggies.

Grow what is not readily available at the market. This includes heirloom and classic varieties, and uncommon (and often expensive) herbs and spices.

Planting varieties of herbs and tomatoes will give your garden lovely color and "foliage."

GARDENS **349**

611

Brighten your home in winter and save money by growing culinary herbs like mint, basil, parsley, and bay.

612

Compensate for the dry air of winter by placing pots in a waterproof tray filled with pebbles and water.

High-bush blue-
berries, for example,
not only present
lovely foliage and
fall color, but
produce a crop of
delicious fruit.

Growing with Cold Frames

614 Save money and get a head start on spring planting with seedlings grown in a cold frame, a boxlike construction with a glass or plastic cover that retains passive solar warmth.

615 Put hardier varieties—like broccoli and leeks—outdoors first, and experiment with one or two plants before moving out your whole crop.

616 Cold frames can be constructed in many ways. The easiest is to make a frame with bricks or lumber, then cover with an old glass window or door of appropriate size.

617 Install a heating coil inside your cold frame for year-round use.

618 In typical northern U.S. climates, seedlings sprouted indoors can be placed in the cold frame starting in late March, as soon as nighttime temperatures begin to stabilize in the 30s.

619 If you live in a very cold climate, it is best to dig the level of the cold-frame plantings eight inches or so below the ground level.

620 Use a cold frame as well to grow hardy fresh herbs throughout the winter.

❧ Wildflower Gardens

621 Most gardeners are amazed to find that they can grow as many as a thousand flowers from five dollars worth of seed.

622 Plant wildflowers in a well-drained spot with loose soil, one that receives at least eight hours of direct sunlight a day.

623 For an inexpensive and low-maintenance garden area, consider growing wildflowers.

Rake or till the top-soil to no more than one inch deep and broadcast the wild-flower seeds evenly. Hint: to facilitate even distribution of the seed, mix one part seed to four parts of a "carrier" such as potting soil.

Press seeds down gently by walking or rolling, and keep seeds moist until they germinate in ten to twenty-five days.

Wildflowers are not only beautiful and virtually mainte-nance free, they help stem erosion, eliminate the need for mowing, and provide a habitat for birds, bees, and butterflies.

Shade Gardens

Those who do not own vast estates with open sunny meadows at every turn must deal with the shade created by neighboring structures and the tall trees we love. However, by paying close attention to various growing conditions and species appropriate for each, you can have satisfying plantings throughout your property.

Deep shade refers to an area that receives no direct sunlight or just an hour or two at the beginning or end of the day. Partial shade refers to an area that receives only three to four hours of direct sunlight a day, or dappled light, such as under a tree.

629
Pay close attention to labels on the nursery stock you purchase; then plant accordingly and you will not lose any. While full-shade-loving plants will tolerate the increased light of partial shade, the reverse is rarely true.

Shade gardens need nutrients, the cheapest and easiest of which is leaf mold, the composted remains of last year's raking. Layer your leaves with ammonium nitrate every few inches to speed the process of decomposition.

Growing Flowers

631 Window boxes are by far the most economical way to dress up your home in a palette that pleases, or, if you crave variety, a different color scheme every year.

632 Use a prefertilized soil mix (made from peat moss and vermiculite) for its light weight and to keep plants thriving all summer.

633 Give your boxes a good soaking twice a day in the hottest summer months.

634 Choose plants with extended blooming periods, and select a variety of growing shapes—some that will grow upright and others that will hang.

635 Plant first in light-weight plastic liners. Not only will they prevent the wooden boxes from rotting, they can be removed to be worked on or to "rest" in an out of the way growing area.

636
Cut flowering peach branches before a late-arriving winter blast takes them away.

637
Mix pussy willow, anemones, primroses, and fragrant lily of the valley to brighten up a window.

638
By cutting branches in succession, you can prolong the show over several weeks.

639

You've invested too much time and energy in your landscape and plantings not to take the earliest advantage of them. Cut the earliest spring blooms for display inside to stretch the floral season to the maximum.

640

Keep tulips in a cold place, and recondition the water and trim stems every few days.

641

Once indoors, remove all but the uppermost leaves, recut the stems on the diagonal, and arrange in a vase filled with fresh water and a floral preservative.

642

Planting as many tulip bulbs as possible in autumn will bring you a reward come spring. Prolong the life and beauty of your cut tulips by following some simple steps.

643

Cut flowers early in the morning and submerge in a bucket of warm water and a floral preservative, easily made by adding a capful of bleach and two teaspoons of sugar to a gallon of water.

644

For a rustic and stylish display, tuck potted hyacinth and primrose into a gardening pail or galvanized bucket.

645

A long list of flowering bushes and trees—from forsythia and cherry to pear and ornamental quince—can be forced into early bloom indoors.

Outdoor Living

646

An impromptu tent made of lightweight fabric slung over steel poles provides shade for dining outdoors; adding candles or lanterns at night creates a magical atmosphere.

647

A hammock can be doubly relaxing
when paired with a flea-market side
table to hold drinks, snacks, and
reading materials.

648

An antique mirror with a repainted frame allows beautiful outdoor scenery to be viewed in any direction.

649 Use furniture, plantings, and architectural garden elements to help divide a small yard into a series of intimate outdoor "rooms."

650

Conserve water by dousing your lawn and plants in the morning or evening. Water is lost more quickly when the sun is high.

651

Nothing beats an outdoor shower for cooling down and cleaning up after a hot day working in the garden. A budget fixture can be set up with parts from the hardware store attached to your hose.

652

A sprinkler set up to moisten paved surfaces will cool the surrounding air and ground through evaporation and make going barefoot a pleasure.

653
Capture more living space economically with a pergola, which instantly defines an outdoor area for dining or relaxing.

654

For colorful patio
seating, paint
inexpensive
wooden chairs
in bright and
contrasting
colors.

Blend the indoors with the outdoors by adding fabric to the patio area. New durable fabrics for curtains and pillows can take the sun and even some rain.

656

For serving ease, use a colorful child's wagon to transport a bucket of ice-cold drinks to guests on far-flung lawn chairs.

A decorative planter made of fiberglass is an inexpensive (under $30) alternative to the handmade ceramic glazed piece ($160).

658

While flowers and shrubs are ephemeral, changing with the seasons, paving is the ultimate perennial.

The colors and textures of your outdoor building materials will determine the mood and feel of your outdoor "room."

660
Change the shape and feel of your walkways by utilizing movable potted plants.

661
Bricks come in many sizes, shapes, colors, and textures. Lay out a few and live with them for a while before making a final decision.

Do-It-Yourself Projects

Doing it yourself has multiple rewards: the pleasure of seeing your project develop as you intended, the well-deserved pride you feel when friends or family comment on your achievement, and, in keeping with our budget theme, the satisfaction of having saved some money—a resource that can be applied to advancing other decorating goals.

In fact, "do it yourself" is often a bit of a misnomer. Why not do it with friends or with family members? Although a shared craft project might result in whimsical party decorations, it could also produce a treasured family heirloom. Here are a variety of projects that use objects readily collected or found in most households—from beads, buttons, and beach finds to fabrics, flowers, and frames.

Painting and Distressing

662

Painted floors were typical of Colonial interiors. With a little work and care, this look can easily be recreated. The floor should be cleaned and sanded first.

663

After laying down the paler shade and letting it dry, mark lines with a yardstick and pencil. Mask off the spaces not to be painted with self-adhesive vinyl diamonds cut to fit your dimensions (these are twelve by twenty-five inches). Paint between the diamonds with your darker color.

664

Painted floors need not be fussed over. Irregularities and wear add character.

665

Special combing tools and brushes can also be used to create dramatic effects.

Applying paint in creative ways can lead to a variety of interesting surface features. Anything from crunched-up plastic bags to feathers to sea sponges can be used to get an effect that pleases.

Colors can be daubed on to reflect the texture and shape of the applicator, or can be rubbed or wiped to create new effects.

Above all, practice your technique on a sample board to make sure you will be happy with the results before tackling a whole wall or room.

669
You can inexpensively give new furniture that sought-after distressed look. All you need is paint in two colors, a metal scraper, a paraffin stick, and some sandpaper.

670
Apply the base coat with a foam brush and let dry. Rub paraffin spots here and there over the piece, then apply the second color of paint overall.

When dry, use the scraper and sandpaper to remove some of the top coat of paint; it comes off easily where the paraffin has been applied, creating the distressed finish.

Continue sanding lightly, paying attention especially to places that would naturally have been more well worn.

New Uses for Vintage Fabrics

673 The hunt for vintage fabrics is only half the fun. Giving them new roles, decorative or functional, provides a thrill all its own.

674 Transform antique linens and cotton hankies into accent pillows. Detail with shell buttons, hand crocheted trim, and embroidery.

675 Use ruffles and eyelet trimming to soften the lines of form-fitting cotton slipcovers.

Tea-Dyed Linens

676
For those drawn to the nostalgic look of aged textiles (or perhaps have a stash of stained linens) dyeing fabrics in tea adds character and color.

677
Presoak the fabric and add to a dye made from boiling water with from four to twenty tea bags (depending upon the size of the piece).

678
Control the degree of dyeing by varying steeping times, from fifteen minutes to overnight.

679
Rinse the dyed fabric thoroughly in cold water with a tablespoon of white vinegar to set the color. Dry in the sun or in a clothes dryer.

680

For projects calling for substantial lengths of fabric, vintage reproduction prints provide a period look and a guarantee that enough can be found.

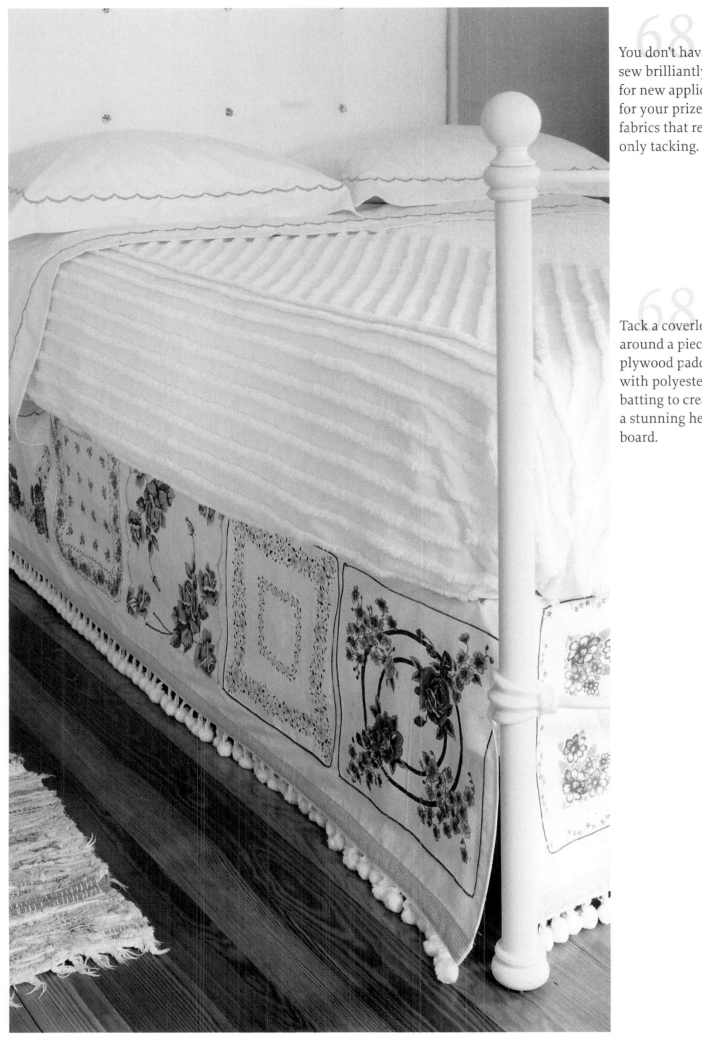

681

You don't have to sew brilliantly. Look for new applications for your prized fabrics that require only tacking.

682

Tack a coverlet around a piece of plywood padded with polyester batting to create a stunning headboard.

683

Pinned up with thumbtacks, a length of flirty floral makes a stylish pantry covering or café curtain.

684

Geometric prints from the fifties look original and sophisticated when framed.

685

Showcase a collection of printed handkerchiefs by using them to make a dust ruffle. Top stitch them along midweight cotton panels attached to a bed sheet. Finish with ball fringe.

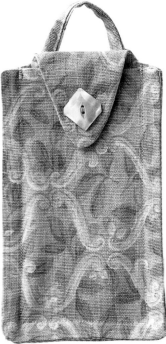

Play with different colors and print combinations and you'll find that well-worn pieces combine gracefully with the new, a look that will continue to evolve as your collection grows.

687

Turn threadbare vintage fabrics into pretty accessories, anything from laundry bags to eyeglass cases. Your only limit is your imagination.

DO-IT-YOURSELF PROJECTS **397**

688

A patchwork throw is a basic and satisfying sewing project, as well as an inexpensive and creative way to add the colors you love to any room. Prewash, press and lay out the fabrics you choose to ensure a dramatic finished quilt.

Ticking is inexpensive and always looks fresh and clean. These red and blue patchwork throw pillows are easily made by sewing four 8 1/2-inch ticking remnants to create sixteen-inch square pillow faces.

690

A lampshade can be covered with fabric by sewing a lower seam on a piece of fabric as long as the shade's circumference. Adding a drawstring seam at the top edge allows it to be pulled in to fit the shade.

Embellish a shelf with ribbon ruffle. Measure the length of the shelf and add five inches. Cut a length of wire-edged craft ribbon to size. Apply a length of double-sided tape to the shelf's edge. Attach the ribbon to the tape and fold it back as you go to create a pretty flounce.

Holiday Decorations

692

Save on holiday decorations by making your own fresh wreaths for display.

Boxwood won't shed needles and ages beautifully; it will stay green as it dries, long beyond the holiday season.

694

To make a simple holiday wreath, wrap green florist's wire around the ends of boxwood clippings to form four or five small bunches. Wrap the bunches around a wreath base so that they overlap.

695

Use your homemade wreaths to decorate shelves, punctuated with jewel-toned ornaments or other trinkets.

696

Use boughs or small trees in stands to decorate bedrooms and give them the scent and color of pine.

697

Colorful produce and garden finds can add spice to decorative winter greenery, as with a star-burst of spiraling kumquats.

698

When fashioning wreaths your imagination is your only limit. Try eye-popping chilies and green apples, or blend flowers, berries, and bundled cinnamon sticks.

Sometimes two wreaths are better than one.

700

Antique rag balls were made by thrifty seamstresses of an earlier era as a way of recycling fabric remnants as useful decorations and playthings. If you can find them at a flea market, remember that the larger ones can be a little heavyfor small Christmas trees. Look for smaller balls, or use them on the thickest branches of your tree.

Lightweight rag balls suitable for use as tree ornaments can be made by wrapping fabric strips around Styrofoam balls. Pins stuck through decorative cutouts serve to hold the fabric in place.

Arranging and Preserving Flowers

702 Magnify the hues of gifts from the garden with a kaleidoscope of colored pencils hot-glued to a glass jar.

703 Fill the jar with your favorite blossoms (we chose purple and white lilacs, anemone, and privet berry), and tie a bow near the bottom.

704 For inexpensive and personalized decorative embellishments, arrange your favorite blooms in easy-to-make color-coordinated containers.

705 Cluster pink peonies and tulips, red roses, and chartreuse verbena in an oversized square vase wrapped in striped and polka-dotted ribbons. Hot-glue the backs of the ribbons to adhere them to the vase.

706 Use sparkling elasticized beaded bracelets (five dollars for a set of six at a costume jewelry store) to encircle an old canning jar. Here, purple and pink hues echo fresh-from-the-garden purple delphiniums and lavender hydrangea blossoms.

707

Economy is the art of preventing waste and making good things last. You can extend the life of those wonderful cut flowers through drying and preserving techniques.

708

Several species, such as roses, hydrangeas, lavender, and straw flowers, can be preserved by simply hanging them upside down in bunches

709

Other flowers are best dried with aid of silica gel, found at craft stores.

Lilacs, roses, peonies, sunflowers, salvia, and zinnias are great for drying and make spectacular table decorations. The few flowers that don't dry well are those with soft, velvety, water-filled blossoms, such as irises and daffodils.

Dried flowers provide color and comfort; on long winter nights, you'll appreciate this wonderful souvenir of summer's bounty.

To preserve blooms, place the flowers in sealable plastic containers; nestle the blossoms in the gel and sprinkle liberally with more gel. Experiment with drying times, which can very from seven days to three weeks.

713

To create inexpensive decorations with a personal touch, transfer the elegant designs and bright colors of flowers directly onto ribbons, cloth, and paper objects.

714

Place strong-hued fresh flowers like pansies or ferns face down on the object you wish to embellish, which should be placed on a sturdy cutting board protected by paper toweling.

715

Place another single layer of paper toweling over the flower and secure all with adhesive tape. Then pound with a small, flat-faced hammer.

Carefully remove
the top layer of
towels and flower
petals with a craft
knife. Run a warm
iron over the image
to set.

717
Budget-conscious decorators passionate about botanical themes should try drying and mounting their own ferns.

718
Place the fronds between two layers of absorbent paper and add weight for a few days. Remove paper and allow ferns to complete drying (a week or longer).

Dryopteris
erythrosora

"...wort"

"Autumn
Fern"

Glue the dried
fronds to museum-
quality mounting
board and frame
appropriately.

 # Picture Frames

720 Create a practical organizer by cutting strips of mat board and gluing, top to bottom, over a full-sized mat board and mounting in a frame.

721 For a decorative effect, use seam-stress's tape to edge the top of each pocket.

722 Paint an assortment of empty picture frames of differing sizes and styles with white acrylic or latex and hang them as a group on a colored wall for graphic effect.

723 A large, ornate frame makes a great bulletin board for a child's' room or home office.

 # Seasonal Crafts

724 Make a ribbon cascade by knotting ribbons of varying lengths and colors first to a smaller top ring, then to a larger ring about 6 inches below it.

725 Finish by pinning fresh or dried blossoms to the ribbons and hanging the cascade over the dining room table.

726 Celebrate the season by filling your home with small, tasteful arrangements of fresh blooms in shades of purple.

727 Show off spring's most fragrant offerings—sprigs of colorful lilacs in glass jars placed on windowsills or side tables are nature's finest potpourri.

Beach Finds

728

Transform a collection of drift-wood into a nautical collage.

For budget decorating calculated to recall breezy summers at the shore, try incorporating your beach finds into whimsical memorabilia.

730 Seashells make charming napkin rings when tied to colorful lengths of string.

Personalized favorite stones make rustic place markers.

732

Put together a display of shells and souvenirs you've collected from the shore.

733

Coat wave-polished rocks with baby oil and display them in a bowl—they'll look as though they just washed up on shore.

734

Store sand from each beach you visit— look for variety of colors and textures—in individual glass bottles.

Comb the beach for color. Sea glass— wave-smoothed remnants of cast- away glass objects— makes a nautical display when paired with driftwood or placed in a bowl of water.

✿ Buttons

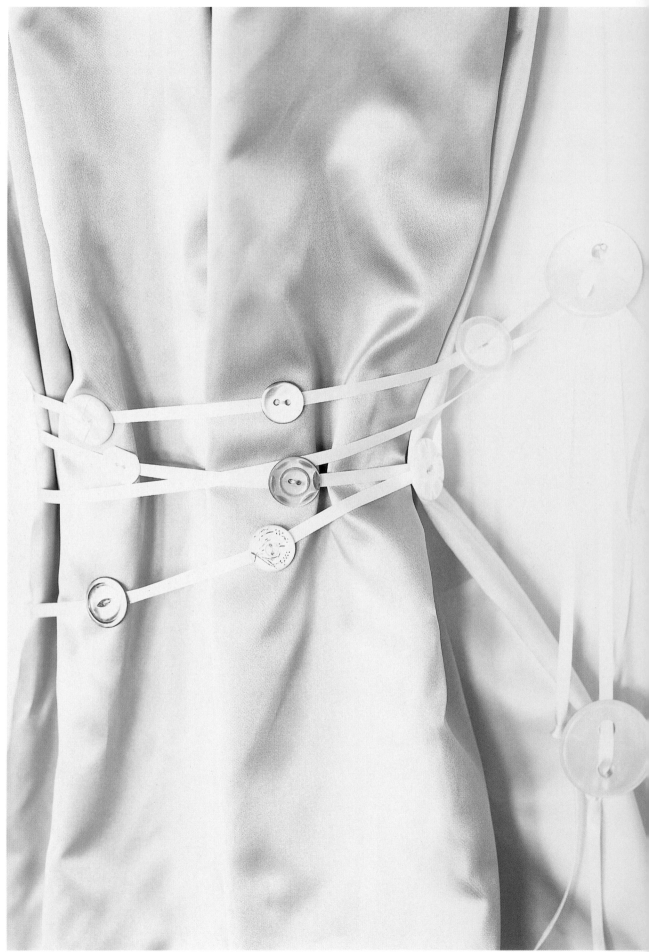

736
Open up your stashed-away button tin and use your imagination to put those vintage treasures to practical and elegant use.

737
Tie back curtains using a ten-foot roll of narrow ribbon—here, double-faced satin—through buttons sewn on at random intervals. Use larger buttons at each end, tacking one to the wall and winding the other end around it.

738 Punch holes in envelopes and weave thin, elegant ribbons to form tie closures. Fasten a button with glue at one end, wrapping the other end of ribbon around it to close the envelope.

739 Use these special envelopes for party invitations or special announcements—they are more personal and less pricey than most store-bought stationery.

740
Sew a pair or small
collection of buttons
to a fabric swatch
and frame for
a focal point.

741
Fill decorative bowls
with vintage buttons in
different colors. The
many shapes, sizes, hues,
and styles of buttons
make a bright, intriguing
display. You could also
put them in glass jars
and line a windowsill or
bookshelf to add color to
an otherwise neutral
space.

742

A collection of vintage buttons can be used for any number of exciting craft projects. Use buttons to adorn a throw pillow, a fifties-style apron, belts—the possibilities are endless!

Handcrafted Journals

743
Secure a scrolled poem or quotation with a length of raffia, ribbon, or string threaded through a miniature trinket, such as a button or shell.

744
Make your record of special events more personal and elegant, either for use as a family keepsake or to give as a present.

A personalized blank journal makes a thoughtful present. Cover the front of a blank book with an exciting fabric; hand stitch initials onto a second, smaller piece and attach by gluing or sewing.

746 Add foliage, water-color paintings, pressed flowers, or careful sketches of your garden or walk to make a beautiful and cherished memento.

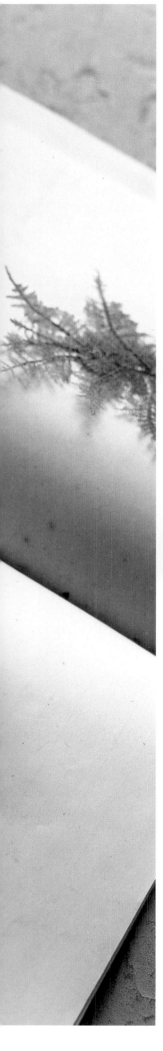

747 A concertina-style journal perfectly records the findings of a family nature walk. Weave strips of ribbon through holes evenly punched into either side of thick paper cards and attach finds with dressmaker's pins or glue.

748 As an easy alternative to scrapbooking, capture the season in a memory box, filled with mementos and photos and decorated with a personal touch.

Knitting

Knitting seems a more popular hobby than ever before and offers many inexpensive and dramatic decorating possibilities. Here a hand-knit afghan in an intricate "basket of flowers" design makes the back of a chair more interesting.

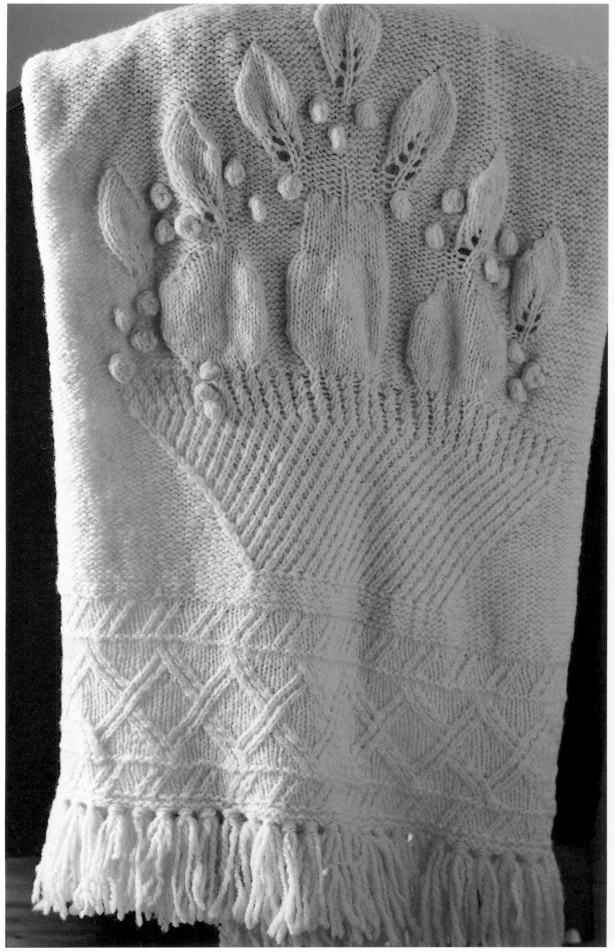

Your knitting projects and even the materials themselves can make a colorful focal point when nicely arranged. Hang scarves from a folding rack and colorful skeins of yarn from pegs on a cork board.

❧ Photography Credits

Pages 6–7 Peter Christopher/Masterfile

Page 8 Peter Margone

Page 11 Peter Margone

Page 12 Gridley &Graves

Pages 14–15 Gridley &Graves

Page 16 John Gruen

Page 16–17 William P. Steele

Page 18 Keith Scott Morton

Page 19 Courtesy of IFLOOR.COM

Page 19 John Bessler

Pages 20–22 Gridley & Graves

Page 23–24 Keith Scott Morton

Page 25 Steve Gross and Sue Daly

Pages 26–27 Keith Scott Morton

Page 28–32 William P. Steele

Page 33 Andrew McCaul

Page 33 Anastassios Mentis

Page 34–35 Keith Scott Morton

Page 35 Anastassios Mentis

Page 36 William P. Steele

Pages 36–37 Pierre Chanteau

Page 37 William P. Steele

Pages 38–39 Jonn Coolidge

Page 40 John Gruen

Page 40 Gridley & Graves

Page 41 Steven Randazzo

Page 42 Keith Scott Morton

Pages 42–43 Susan Gentry McWhinney

Page 44 Michael Luppino

Page 45 Natasha Milne

Page 46 John Bessler

Page 48 Steven Randazzo

Page 49 Keith Scott Morton

Pages 50–51 Keith Scott Morton

Page 51 (right) John Gruen

Page 52 Keith Scott Morton

Page 53 Steven Randazzo

Page 54 (top) John Bessler

Page 54 (bottom) Steven Randazzo

Page 55 Keith Scott Morton

Page 56 Andrew McCaul

Page 57–59 Steven Randazzo

Page 60 Debi Treloar

Page 61 Steven Randazzo

Page 62 John Gruen

Page 63 (top) Chris Scott

Page 63 (bottom) Keith Scott Morton

Page 64 Jonn Coolidge

Page 66 Tham Nu Tran

Page 67–69 Keith Scott Morton

Pages 70–71 David Prince

Pages 72–73 Keith Scott Morton

Page 74–75 Michael Weschler

Page 76 (top) Keith Scott Morton

Page 76 (bottom) Keith Scott Morton

Page 77 Courtesy of Broyhill Furniture Industries

Pages 78–79 Tom Leighton

Page 80 David Prince

Page 81 Charlie Colmer

Page 82 Gridley & Graves

Pages 82–83 David Prince

Page 84 Debi Treloar

Page 84 Keith Scott Morton

Pages 84–85 Anne Gridley &Gary Graves

Pages 86–87 David Prince

Pages 88–89 Jim Bastardo

Page 90–91 Anastassio Mentis

Pages 92–96 Keith Scott Morton

Page 97 Michael Luppino

Pages 98–99 Gridley & Graves

Page 100–101 Gridley & Graves

Page 101 Steven Randazzo

Page 102 Pierre Chanteau

Page 103–104 Dasha Wright

Page 105 Dasha Wright

Page 105 Michael Weschler

Page 106–107 Caroline Arber

Page 108 (top) Caroline Arber

Page 108 (bottom) Sandra Lane/Country Homes
     & Interiors

Page 109 Jessie Walker

Page 110 David Prince

Page 111 (top) Keith Scott Morton

Page 111 (bottom) Anne Gridley & Gary Graves

Page 112 Rob Melnychuk

Page 114 Michael Luppino

Page 115–117 John Bessler

Page 118–119 Andrew McCaul

Page 120 Tom Leighton

Page 121 Andrew McCaul

Page 122 (top) David Prince

Page 122 (bottom) Keith Scott Morton

Page 123 Paul Wicheloe

Page 124 (top) Alex Ramsay

Page 124 (bottom) Anne Gridley & Gary Graves

Page 125–129 Keith Scott Morton

Page 130 Andrew McCaul

Page 131 Helen Norman

Page 132 Andrew McCaul

Page 133 (top) Pierre Chanteau

Page 133 (bottom) Keith Scott Morton

Page 134–141 Keith Scott Morton

Page 142 Caroline Arber

Page 143 (top) Dennis Kurkowski

Page 143 (bottom) Keith Scott Morton

Page 144 (top) Simon Upton

Pages 144–145 Keith Scott Morton

Page 146 William P. Steele

Page 147 Dennis Kurkowski

Page 148 Keith Scott Morton

Page 150–151 Steven Mays

Page 152–153 Keith Scott Morton

Pages 154–155 Anne Gridley & Gary Graves

Page 156 (top left) courtesy of Pulaski Furniture

Pages 157–165 Keith Scott Morton

Page 166 Jonn Coolidge

Page 167 Paul Wicheloe

Page 168 Helen Norman

Page 169 Amy Neunsinger/Getty Images

Page 170–171 Caroline Arber

Page 172 Keith Scott Morton

Page 174 Natasha Milne

Page 175 (top) Courtesy of Crate & Barrel

Page 175 (bottom) Courtesy of Retrospect

Page 176 Evan Bracken

Page 177 (top) Jim Bastardo

Page 177 (bottom) Evan Bracken

Page 178 (top) Evan Bracken

Page 178 (bottom) Tom Leighton

Page 179 Evan Bracken

Page 180 Paul Whicheloe

Page 181 Paul Whicheloe

Page 182–183 Chuck Baker

Page 184 Courtesy of JC Penney

Page 185 Keith Scott Morton

Page 186 William P. Steele

Page 187 Keith Scott Morton

Page 188–193 David Prince

Page 194 (top) Keith Scott Morton

Page 194 (bottom) Courtesy of Maytag

Page 195 (top) Keith Scott Morton

Page 195 (bottom) Susan Gentry McWhinney

Page 196–201 Keith Scott Morton

Pages 202–205 Dennis Kurkowski

Page 206 Michael Luppino

Page 208 (top left) Ann Hobgood

Page 209–210 Courtesy of Preservation North Carolina

Page 211 (upper right) Weldon Jenkins

Page 212 William P. Steele

Page 213 Keith Scott Morton

Page 214 (top) Adrien Briscoe

Page 214 (bottom) Christopher Drake

Page 215 Michael Luppino

Page 216 (top) Anne Gridley & Gary Graves

Page 217 William P. Steele

Page 218–219 William P. Steele

Page 219 Evan Bracken

Page 220–223 Ericka McConnell

Page 224 Steven Randazzo

Page 225 (top) Courtesy of Period Lighting Fixtures, Inc.

Page 225 (bottom) Andrew McCaul

Page 226 (top) Grey Crawford

Page 226 (bottom) Jonn Coolidge

Page 227 Michael Luppino

Page 228 Keith Scott Morton

Page 229 (top right) Eric Crichton/Garden
    Picture Library

Page 230 (top left) Ron Sutherland/Garden
    Picture Library

Page 231 Marge Garfield

Page 232–233 Keith Scott Morton

Page 234–235 Anne Gridley & Gary Graves

Pages 358–361 Rick Wetherbee
Page 362–363 John Peden
Page 364 Caroline Arber
Page 365 Pia Tryde
Page 366 Digital Vision/Picture Quest
Page 366 Rick Wetherbee
Page 367–368 Pia Tryde
Page 369 Craig Fordham
Page 370–371 Keith Scott Morton
Page 371 Jonn Coolidge
Page 372 Jessie Walker
Page 376 Andrew McCaul
Page 377 Keith Scott Morton
Pages 374–375 Andrew McCaul
Pages 376–377 Gridley & Graves
Page 378 Steven Randazzo
Page 379 (top and middle right): Dasha Wright
Page 379 (bottom left and right): Andrew McCaul)
Page 380–381 Gridley & Graves
Page 382–383: Ron Sutherland/Garden
        Picture Library
Page 384 David Prince
Page 386–387 Steven Randazzo
Pages 388–389 Keith Scott Morton
Page 390–391 Jonn Coolidge
Page 392–393 Steven Randazzo
Page 393 (bottom) Caroline Arber
Page 394–395 Jonn Coolidge

Page 396–397 Jonn Coolidge
Pages 398–399 Colin McGuire
Page 400–401 David Brittain
Page 402–403 David Prince
Page 404 David Prince
Page 405 Jeff McNamara
Page 406–407 Marie–Louise Avery
Page 408–409 Keith Scott Morton
Page 410–411 Andrew McCaul
Page 412 Rick Wetherbee
Page 413 John Glover
Page 414 Steven Mays
Page 415 Rob Gray
Page 416–417 Dasha Wright Ewing
Page 418–419 Andrew McCaul
Page 420 Debi Treloar
Page 421 Steve Gross & Sue Daly
Page 422–423 Caroline Arber
Page 424 Steven Randazzo
Page 425 Susan Gentry
Page 426 David Montgomery
Page 427 Lisa Romerein/Getty Images
Page 428–429 Susan Gentry
Page 430 (top) Susan Gentry
Page 430 (bottom) Steven Randazzo
Page 431 Steven Randazzo
Page 432–435 Kate Gadsby
Page 436–437 Michael Luppino

❧ Index